WOKE

AN ANESTHESIOLOGIST'S VIEW

MADHAVA K. SETTY, MD

To : Galileo di Vincenzo Bonaulti de Galilei

"Believe nothing, no matter where you read it or who has said it, not even if I have said it, unless it agrees with your own reason and your own common sense."

—The Buddha

TABLE OF CONTENTS

FOREWORD

Whether you are aware of it or not, we are in the midst of a planetary awakening, and for many it can be a very confusing time. Rather than adding yet another opinion to the noise, Dr. Setty instead introduces the fascinating possibility that we are being called to rely upon our own intuition to guide us through this remarkable transition.

It is difficult to do justice to what is presented here. I invite you to plant your feet on solid ground and open yourself to an amazingly rigorous, thoughtful and often entertaining exploration into our minds and our history. This unique book will prove to be a potent source of comfort and wisdom to those who are ready. "Woke" is a primer for a new age on this planet.

—Jim McCarty, scribe for the Ra contact

ACKNOWLEDGEMENTS

I will forever be indebted to all my teachers, especially to those who have appeared disguised as my patients and family members. I am deeply grateful to Jill, my wife, for her insight, undying support and irrepressible passion for life.

PROLOGUE

"Woke" has undeniably become a charged word. It is most commonly used to describe perspectives that stress the importance of acknowledging systemic racism, sexism, gender inequality and other prejudices that exist in our society whether overtly or not. More recently it has been appropriated by various movements to proclaim their greater awareness of "the truth", whatever that truth may be. By doing so those who hold these "woke" perspectives claim moral or intellectual superiority over those who do not. This predictably results in pushback from others who see things differently and find the use of the word insulting. In that sense "woke" is now giving rise to division and not unity.

Here I seek to resurrect what can be considered the "original" sense of the word, if there ever was one. An "awake" mind, at least in the way it was attributed to a certain individual we know as the Buddha, was one that was free of delusion. Being "awake" in this sense is not associated with any religion or ideology. It is merely a state of seeing things as they are. No superiority is claimed. There is no punishment for not buying in. Being "woke", as it was originally used, was rather an invitation to consider a fascinating possibility: a mind free of delusion *suffers less*. In other words, when seen clearly, reality itself is compassionate.

Could this really be true? To loosely quote the Buddha, "You have to see it for yourself." At the surface it seems that accepting this invitation is a mixed bag. Of course nobody wants to suffer more than they have to, but who wants to admit that they are deluded to begin with? In any case, how could a deluded person ever recognize themselves as such?

One way is to notice the presence of suffering. If there is suffering, it could be a product of "delusion" as the Buddha suggested. However, accepting that as an answer requires you to buy into this whole system of thought to begin with. Another way is to look at it from the opposite end: if you are certain that you are not deluded, I would propose that *certainty is in fact a product of a deluded mind*. But why should you believe *that*? Looking at it openly there isn't any real logic in accepting this invitation. If you agree I suggest that you are actually seeing things quite clearly. What the Buddha was offering was nothing more than a paradigm. However once accepted, he claimed that it led to something much more than a system of thought.

Taking the step towards this idea of "wokeness" is done out of sheer curiosity. Curiosity is an element of the human mind that we spend little time cultivating these days, and it is having serious consequences. Curiosity represents the dynamic aspect of our intelligence. Without it, how would we ever expand our understanding of anything? Instead we have placed increasing emphasis on finding narratives that resonate with our "truths" and fiercely defending them without diligently examining the basis of that truth first. Can there be any better evidence of this than the degradation of the respect people once had for those who held differing opinions from them? It is not anyone's fault. Rather we are witnessing a subtle but perceptible change in our minds *collectively*. What were once "differing opinions" slowly became "alternative beliefs" that are now being proclaimed as "individual truths". Most of us can attest to the challenges of openly discussing a topic with someone who regards their position as "their truth". Is it reasonable to think that there can be as many "truths" as there are people? Or are we becoming utterly confused because we are unable to recognize the *uncertainty* in our positions?

This is not a book about meditation, Buddhism or New-Age philosophy. It is an attack on conventional "wisdom" and requires you, the reader, to fully engage your intellect at times and drop it completely at others. Why would we ever want to drop our intellect if we are trying to get to the bottom of things? The answer is that our intellect can only take us so far. A sharpened intellect can efficiently dismiss lines of reasoning that will lead to inaccurate conclusions while at the same time acknowledge its own limited capacity to *fully* understand anything. Acknowledging this limitation is in fact what keeps it engaged and firing on all cylinders. I propose that a well-honed intellect may get us very close but not all the way. We must engage another power, intuition, to take the final steps. The confusion around us today is a result of relying on intuition too early, too often or never at all.

This book is an exploration into the idea of certainty. I contend that we have been using the term carelessly by attributing it to things we *presume* to know. By doing so we are severely crippling our ability to expand our understanding of our world and ourselves. Our minds are growing more static. Nature has always been reminding us that we live in a dynamic world. Seasons change, tectonic plates shift, the very axis of our planet's rotation is wobbling. What happens to a mind that is fixated on a given understanding of a world that is in constant flux? Suffering perhaps?

My approach to challenging this idea of certainty is simple. I forego topics where we differ greatly in our opinions (politics, religion, government, choice of news sources, etc) and focus on those where we have the most consensus: death, money and war. These are unavoidable parts of the human experience. These are the *presumed* certainties. They may be unavoidable, but are they really what we think they are? I suggest that we are perpetuating stories about these things because of the trust we have placed in others. In that sense, we have gotten very good at *believing* others while losing our ability to *know* for ourselves. Nobody told the Buddha what to believe. He saw for himself and *knew*.

Our ideas surrounding these topics are so deeply entrenched in our psyche that it would be futile to simply present counter arguments to those we use to defend our position on them. Instead I first explore how our minds arrive at conclusions in a general sense by considering such things as bias and intuition. We are all familiar with these terms but few have closely examined them and the power they have to conceal and reveal reality. This provides a framework to examine how we, as a species, have historically kept ourselves in the dark for tragically long periods.

Finally I directly challenge our ideas of death, money and war by offering alternative explanations to those we hold so tightly. This is the most challenging part of the book to absorb. It gets technical and very detailed. At least one of my counter arguments is widely considered to be a dangerous "conspiracy theory" by societal standards today. Many will choose to look no further. This is not a calculated risk I am choosing to take as the author of this book. It is a necessary part of any serious investigation that seeks to shed light upon deeply held beliefs. Not all conspiracy theories are true, but are you *certain* that they are all false? If you are certain about this I respect your right to disagree. You may still find considerable value in the rest of the book, especially if you are curious.

In the end I hope to offer you a completely different model of how these three "certainties" are interrelated in the world and *in our minds*. It is a *paradigm*. It is just a system of beliefs but when we subscribe to it very big things happen. I propose that the world we live in today is actually a product of a paradigm that we have collectively chosen by default. That paradigm is built from our ideas about death, money and war. If our understanding of these three things change we will end up with an entirely different paradigm and an entirely different world too. In other words, I am inviting you to consider another fascinating possibility: our paradigm is not built from immutable truths about the world, it is the other way around. We have built a world based on paradigms that we have chosen, often for reasons that may not be readily apparent. This idea is also a paradigm--a paradigm about paradigms if you will. It is just a system of thought. Once accepted it may lead to something much more.

Ultimately you decide which model to subscribe to. There is no "right" choice and there are no certainties. Therein lies the beauty of reality. You always have the freedom to choose. However, in order to choose, you must first see that you have a choice to begin with. Is it worth considering this possibility? What might you lose by looking further? How does that compare with what might be lost if you don't?

PREFACE

In 2007 Joshua Bell, a globally recognized virtuoso of the violin, conducted an experiment. He appeared unannounced in a Washington DC subway station dressed inconspicuously in a baseball hat and began to play his 3 million dollar Stradivarius for the unsuspecting commuters while a hidden camera recorded the event. He played for 45 minutes and in that time approximately one thousand people (1097 to be exact) passed by. Only a handful of people paused long enough to listen for more than a few seconds. Near the end of his "performance" a woman stopped in her tracks and stood transfixed. She recognized him from his concert at Boston's Symphony Hall three days earlier. More interestingly, a three-year old boy named Evan was immediately drawn to Bell's sublime playing. His mother, in an excusable hurry, had to drag her son from this renowned musician's presence. Evan continued to crane his neck to watch as he was shuttled away.

I played the violin in the fourth grade and have never held a violin in my hands since. If I were to play at Symphony Hall in Boston in a similar experiment I guarantee the results would be far more memorable for the unwitting participants. Music speaks for itself no matter how it is packaged. But how often are we attending to the packaging and not the music? It depends on the circumstances. When Mr. Bell played in the subway station few people noticed. If I were to play in Symphony Hall, I will be unavoidably heard, at least for a minute or two. Packaging Mr. Bell's performance in a D.C. subway station condemned his genius to obscurity. The exquisite acoustics of Boston's symphony hall would do little to enhance the value of what I could offer. The packaging can certainly be important, but in order for music to be truly heard someone must be *listening*.

I had every intention of publishing this book anonymously as an attempt to eliminate any bias that might arise in your mind from packaging it in one way or another. It was to be a different kind of experiment that was designed to offer something to the truly curious. Without any validation from third parties you would have been left with a choice: to explore what is offered here using your own wits or move on to a better use of your time. The manuscript was in its final stages of publication when I had a change of heart. You see, this book explores at least one topic that is extremely controversial and several others that are unequivocally labeled "pseudoscientific" by the very same institutions that confer "legitimacy" to my opinion in our society today. I concluded that it would have been disingenuous, if not cowardly, to not put my name on this book. We are at a moment where transparency and courage is more important than ever before. It is my hope that you will accept or dismiss what is presented here using your own sensibilities and no one else's, including mine.

In this day and age we can find supporting "evidence" of any opinion we choose to entertain, no matter how outrageous. How then can we come to any conclusions about anything? Whether we are comfortable with it or not, we are faced with the reality that we will, at some point, have to place trust in something or someone. Where we decide to place that trust is up to us. In this sense, we must have trust in ourselves before we can trust anyone else. This is not so easy for a population that has grown comfortable deferring to others for nearly all their information, from dietary advice to world events. The intellects of yesteryear, who brought innovation through their unfettered exploration of independent ideas, are nearly gone. Today, "intelligence" is becoming a function of how discerning one is in selecting a *source* of their information and not in the information itself.

We are living in a fascinating world where the media diverge greatly in the manner in which they report the news; we have a Commander in Chief that insists some news is "fake", and "conspiracy theories" and various versions of snake oil salesmen abound. Now, more than ever before, we need to clarify how and why we choose to either accept or dismiss what we are being told.

This book is about sharpening one's insight and intuition. These are powers innate to us and are often unrecognized or ignored. Insight and intuition do not arise from belief in others or their credentials. They arise of their own, in minds that are prepared and free of bias. Without engaging these powers we will continue to go on believing but never *knowing*. This places us in a vulnerable position, especially in an environment in which opinions are being touted as facts and dissenters are subject to personal attacks.

Once we can come to an understanding of what intuition is and what it *feels* like we can then apply it to our understanding of our world and how it works. This entails reexamining some fundamental concepts that have long remained outside of diligent inquiry. Have we been making assumptions? Perhaps. Perhaps making assumptions is unavoidable. If we are making assumptions, *are we making the right ones*? This is where the book gets technical and highly controversial. I propose that we have been making wrong assumptions for a very long time because we have placed trust in others and not in ourselves. The assumptions we have made underpin a paradigm of our world that we hold collectively. It is that paradigm that gives rise to the kind of world we have today. With different assumptions comes a different paradigm. With a different paradigm comes a different world. I propose that when we dutifully engage our intuition when making our assumptions we will create a world far more abundant than we have ever thought possible. That's the payoff for getting controversial.

Although the book has detailed discussions of complex concepts and novel perspectives, it is referenced sparsely. There is little purpose in pointing out concurring opinions about ideas that are intended to stand on their own. Search them out if you wish. You will find them sitting next to those that refute them. Where will that leave you? You could say that this book is not written for the casually curious or indiscriminate. It is for the one in a thousand, for the Evans out there.

INTRODUCTION

Do we know more than we don't know? Obviously the question cannot be answered definitively, but do you have a *gut feeling*?

If we believe the unknown is much larger than that which we know, it may motivate us to redouble our efforts to learn more so that we can find new ways to change our world for the better in ways never previously conceived. For those of us who are driven by curiosity alone, believing the unknown is unimaginably vast offers them the possibility of endless fascination and discovery. For those who are not curious and believe that much of the present situation cannot be changed, such questions are moot. Why devote time and energy to know more if there isn't anything else out there to learn?

Let us examine an analogous situation by substituting "seeing" for "knowing". How did our ancestors discover that they were not able to see all that could be seen? Although their power of sight was quite satisfactory during the daytime, it became obvious that many animals could see more than they could at night. Nocturnal animals seemed perfectly capable of maneuvering in a cloak of darkness while we humans remained confined to the protection of caves or firelight. It would also have been clear that even in broad daylight birds of prey had greater acuity than we humans possessed. Our predecessors surely must have contemplated how the same world appeared to the hawk perched on a nearby tree. It would have been obvious that we were not able to grasp the full picture. But how *much* were we missing?

Our curiosity and desire to improve our conditions drove us to explore the nature of light and the utility of the refractive power of certain materials. Looking glasses eventually allowed us to sight land from afar, telescopes allowed us to examine objects in the sky more closely. Eventually our satellite-based cameras offered a previously unimaginable ability to marvel at phenomena unfolding billions of light years away. Less than twenty years ago the famous Hubble telescope was pointed at one of the darkest parts of our night sky. Painstaking observations made over the course of months resulted in a stunning image, called the Hubble Ultra Deep Field. The image contains 15,000 galaxies, each thousands of light years across. Perhaps more stupefying is that the picture captured only one *26 millionth* of the sky. This is roughly the amount of sky obscured by a pinhead held at an arm's length.

Similarly, microscopes allowed us to survey an entire world right in front of our noses that we didn't know existed. Then came the understanding that visible light was only a tiny window of electromagnetic waves that pervade our universe. Being able to detect other frequencies of radiation allowed us to directly examine the structure of matter and determine the molecular configuration of our own DNA. How much would we have been able to "see" today if our predecessors shrugged off the hawk circling from a mile above?

Given our present understanding that our species is perhaps 200,000 years old and that these advances have all come only in the last 500 years, we must conclude that what remains unseen is far greater than we previously imagined. Why would we assume that in a relative blink of the eye we have completely plumbed the limits of what can be potentially seen?

Our understanding of ourselves, our history and our place in the cosmos has taken a similar trajectory. Yet there exists a growing sense of complacency amongst us. The presumption that we have already explained nearly everything no longer seems as far-fetched as it may have 1000 years ago when our ancestors gazed at the heavens asking "What's out there?". I am suggesting that this complacency, combined with our automatic deference to "experts" and our unquestioning attitude towards information that happens to resonate with our own poorly investigated "truths" is rapidly impeding our natural growth toward our own potential. What that potential is I would not venture to estimate for I am of the camp that believes what is unknown is literally infinite. No matter how you feel about the size of the unknown, we can agree that we can only work with what we know right now.

In order to see more we had to first recognize our vision was limited before we could endeavor to improve it. Similarly, in order to *know* more it is necessary to recognize that our knowledge is limited *before* we can hope to broaden and deepen our understanding. Research and objective investigation expand our knowledge, but what is it that keeps us from acknowledging that our knowledge is limited in the first place?

This book is an open and diligent examination of the possibility that the greatest impediment to expanding our knowledge is our own limited objectivity. By overestimating the level of understanding we possess right now we limit how much we will understand tomorrow. In other words, any belief that we take as true without open and diligent inquiry will unavoidably prevent us from arriving at a greater understanding. These "cognitive blind spots" are judgements that are made prematurely and are, by definition, *biases.*

How is it possible to know whether we are biased? How can a mind become aware of its own distortions? This is a more fascinating question than it may seem initially. Is there an intuitive knowing that is beyond conceptualization? Perhaps. Many would argue that this kind of intuitive knowing pervades their lives and ultimately defines their world. They would call it faith. To them objectivity only plays a superficial role in getting to the truth. Using facts to overturn a faith-based position is ultimately futile. When facts contradict a belief founded on faith they will inevitably be discarded as inaccurate.

For those of us who instead seek an understanding based in objectivity, the idea of an intuitive knowing can seem potentially dangerous. However objectivity comes with its own difficulties. How can one know if they are being objective? Because we each have an extremely limited set of personal experiences to draw upon yet hold an understanding of reality that is based in everything from cosmology to particle physics and economics to archeology, we must concede that we have had to trust others' experience and opinion. Is that objective? There is nothing wrong with trusting others, but we are not being objective when we do. On what basis do we decide to trust others (individuals and/or massive scientific institutions)? Is it because of their track record of being more or less right? How would we know that they have been getting it right if we have been confined to such limited personal experiences? We must, at some level, be relying on something outside of objectivity.

If this is unclear or not-self evident, consider this question : How do you choose what to believe? If you choose to defer to a textbook, news source or another's opinion, that too is a choice made of your own volition. Either way, you *choose* who or what to believe. On what basis do you make that choice if your choices are in turn based on *what you believe*? As you recursively examine why you believe in something you must eventually arrive at a point where you simply "know" it to be true *independent of the veracity of any other belief*. At that point "knowing" does not require logic but only what can be best described as intuition. If you never arrive at that point in your exploration you must conclude that whatever you believed to be true or false actually falls into the realm of uncertainty. Admitting that you are uncertain about something can be the greatest insight you could ever have.

Something known intuitively could be any belief : one that underpins a complex theory, a worldview or just an isolated fact. In this sense, your *intuition ultimately forms the basis of all that you know*.

If that proposition is disconcerting or seems fanciful to you, consider the fact that in science there are certain principles that are taken to be true *without any explanation*. If you believe that such things do not or should not exist in the realm of science you would be wrong. In fact these inexplicable beliefs form the foundation upon which elaborate theories that explain the nature of the universe are based. These beliefs are, in fact, called *Laws*. Scientific laws are taken to be true despite the fact that there is no known explanation of why they are true, yet without them there would be no basis for any scientific model of reality.

Take the Law of Gravitational Attraction as an example. That there is a gravitational influence between every object in the universe is undisputed. Gravity is the basis of modern cosmology. Gravity is the force that keeps everything we can see with the naked eye from flying apart. This is the force we must overcome to build skyscrapers, to design aircraft, to send satellites into orbit or put a person on the moon. From the time we were stumbling around as toddlers we have become accustomed to living in a world where we are invisibly connected to the ground. We can measure, calculate and predict gravity's effects with incredible accuracy.

As mentioned above, a "law" in science is the term given to a phenomenon that is accepted as true *without any need for explanation*. The next time you are tossing a ball around ask yourself, "Why does it always fall back to the ground?". If you think scientists have an answer to this basic question you would be wrong. We have no idea *why* gravity exists or *how* it exerts effect upon anything with mass. Neither do we have any idea of why opposite charges and magnetic poles attract each other or why protons in an atom stay together. The entire universe, from the molecules that make up our brains to those in supermassive black holes function and interact with everything else based on "laws" of gravity, electromagnetic and nuclear forces. Once accepted as fact, these laws allow us to synthesize intricate and dependable models of a physical reality. What these forces are and how they impart their influence is *unknown*, yet without them we would have nothing more than a rudimentary understanding of our world.

The point here is that there is nothing wrong with building a system of understanding that is based on something that is inexplicable--in fact this is ultimately unavoidable. Science is transparent, openly identifying the inexplicable behind all that is explained. It is this transparency that not only lends the highest level of credibility to scientific "opinion" but also offers a flexibility that can only come from an understanding that what is known is always open to refinement or even a complete overhaul because it is all ultimately based on phenomena that has not been explained.

There is little reason to acknowledge the inexplicable basis of the laws of nature in our day-to-day lives. We can be assured that the light will go on when we hit the switch and that the moon is not going to come plummeting to the Earth anytime soon. However it may not be as wise to dismiss the need for further consideration of the framework that supports our personal beliefs. We rarely explore the *basis* of why we believe what we believe when it comes to the questions that concern us the most like "What is the best for me and my family?", "Who should I trust for my information?", "What is the right course of action for my country?", "Why do I choose or not choose to worship a 'higher' power?". Can there be any better evidence of a lack of rigorous inquiry into these questions than the vast and seemingly insurmountable differences between people regarding these matters? If you assiduously searched for the basis of your opinions regarding these questions you will arrive at basic ideas that you assume to be true because they "feel right". This includes the "feeling" that you have seen enough evidence that further questioning is no longer necessary. This "feeling" is intuition, and it is not to be taken lightly; in fact it should be nurtured if one is truly interested in *knowing*.

Obviously we know how to build a bigger and bigger knowledge base, but is there a way to develop a keener intuition? Intuition can only emerge when conceptual blind spots are seen for what they are and then dissolved. In fact, honing one's intuition can be considered an *unlearning* process--an unlearning of unsubstantiated beliefs. Whether or not you subscribe to the idea of intuition or a non-conceptual means of knowing we can all agree that without dispelling unsubstantiated beliefs real clarity will remain outside of our grasp.

This book does not profess *what* is true; it investigates how we decide what is true. Your conclusions, the *what*, is entirely up to you alone. This is a vitally important distinction to make. Unlike news reports, economic textbooks or religious scripture, this book does not demand that you accept a narrative, an opinion or a system of thought. Instead it offers an invitation to locate assumptions and openly challenge them, perhaps for the first time in many cases. In this sense, this book is offered not to educate but to stimulate.

The early chapters are a series of short stories designed to examine the insidious nature of bias and how it can arise even in the alert mind. The book next explores the role bias has played in our history, in some cases contributing to our survival and in others prolonging intellectual stagnancy--sometimes for embarrassingly long periods of time.

The last two thirds of the book are devoted to a direct assault upon the seemingly incontrovertible positions many of us hold on the topics of death, money and war. These topics are intimately connected not just in the external world but in our minds as well. Armed with new insight into your own mind from the early chapters you may discover that these absolutes are not as absolute as you may have thought. For this reason, I suggest that you consider what is offered in the order in which it is presented. How many assumptions are we making when we uphold the common narrative regarding these topics? Are we biased? If so, why and who is biasing us?

These questions cannot be answered without a diligent examination of our media sources taken as a whole. Our understanding of "what is happening and why" is inescapably dependent upon the accuracy of the sources of media we choose. Yet without the media we as individuals would have no idea what was transpiring on the other side of town let alone the other side of the world. How would we know if we were seeing the whole picture if our media provides the only means of seeing to begin with? We find ourselves in the same predicament as our ancient predecessors. Like them we too are saddled with the responsibility of looking a little harder if we want to see more...

CHAPTER 1:

A Tale of Two Trains

This is a story that takes place in a rural town in America's breadbasket one century ago. Citizens of this hypothetical town lived in a typical agrarian society, farming, tending to their livestock, worshiping at church on Sundays and socializing when time and weather permitted. Everyone tended to get along and everyone did their best to lend a helping hand when one family or another was hit with hardship. Most residents had limited formal education but all knew the ways of the land, how to care for their animals and how to read the weather: skills that could not be learned in fancy East coast colleges. A few did receive higher education but were content with the life that this sort of town offered.

One such person, let us call him Ed, while bored on a certain day after harvest decided to run a little experiment. He noticed that trains of two types ran down the one set of tracks not so far from his home. Trains either carried passengers or freight. It was easy to distinguish between the two because passenger cars were easy to distinguish from the tankers and flatbeds. Ed wondered if the tracks carried more passenger trains or freight trains. Every day at a completely random time he would wander down to the tracks and wait for a train to pass by. He meticulously recorded which kind of train it was in his notebook. He did this for a few weeks and was mildly surprised to notice that there were more passenger trains. After a few months, it became clear that in fact there were five times as many passenger trains than freight trains. Enjoying this kind of "research" he dutifully continued his daily visits to the tracks, excited that with more data his surprising conclusion was even more validated.

Finally, after a year of recording and tallying his results he decided to share this with his friends following church one Sunday. After the usual conversation he let everyone in on the experiment he had been conducting. He brought his notebook to show his results. His friends were mildly curious not just about the results but also of the fact that Ed had taken the time to look into something that had absolutely no bearing on anything practical. That being said, nobody could argue with his findings or his method.

News of this relatively pointless piece of information slowly spread and it became generally known that five times as many passenger trains came through town as freight trains. One day one of Ed's friends casually brought this fact up in conversation at the local eatery. "Ha!", came a response from someone sitting nearby, "You've got your numbers all mixed up!"

"I beg your pardon?", asked Ed's friend, Jack.

"There's no way that there are *that* many more passenger trains than freight trains coming through town. I would know. I live right near the tracks. I look up every time a train goes by and it seems to me there are just as many freight trains as passenger trains!"

Jack replies that this has been looked at very closely by a trusted member of the community and Church who, as a matter of fact, spent time in college. The other guy, Lenny, doesn't budge an inch with his assertion.

Source of Bias #1 : Something to be gained or lost by the outcome

Now at this point, they can either both shrug their shoulders and move on, or things can "escalate". No one is making accusations about the other's political affiliation, choice of religion or character, they are just talking about trains. However Jack, empowered by the data which he has seen, decides to challenge Lenny's conviction to his position by betting $10 on the matter. To Jack's mild delight, Lenny takes the bet. "Okay mister", says Jack, "Let's go prove I'm right!"

Why would Lenny, a farmer with little formal education put money on the line in this situation? It is clear to him that what he is being told is wrong because it completely contradicts his own experience. Lenny knows he is right because he trusts his own eyes. Jack, on the other hand, is equally convinced of his position because he has seen the numbers, trusts Ed and his method and the fact that the entire town, more or less, would side with him.

The two pay a visit to Ed's farm. Lenny is shown Ed's meticulous account which not only indicates which kind of train was seen but also the time at which it passed by. Lenny must concede that there were no errors in arithmetic. Lenny is still incredulous and is unwilling to accept the data. Jack accuses Lenny of "welching" on a bet. Lenny becomes incensed because he would be willing to own up if he could be convinced he was wrong. Yet, he has nothing to back up his position except what he knows from his own experience. Moreover, backing out of an agreement is a serious offense in a community where trust in each other is necessary to survive. Harsh words are exchanged. Jack lets everyone in town know that Lenny should not be trusted because he refuses to believe what everyone knows to be true. Lenny, on the other hand, convinced that he is right, must conclude that the books have been "doctored" and that Ed and Jack had set this all up to exploit him. Lenny finds little sympathy in the community because Ed and Jack have always been model citizens.

The story I am describing is hypothetical yet is unfolding in a reasonable, and by today's standards, almost predictable fashion. There is a widely accepted explanation that is backed by evidence. A contrarian opinion, which in this case does not endanger either side, becomes a divisive issue once something of value is on the line such as credibility, character or money. Accusations get thrown back and forth and a community gets disrupted.

Source of Bias #2: Unwillingness to look closer

Lenny becomes ostracized socially and gets punished for disagreeing with a consensus he feels is wrong. The community begins to suspect that Lenny is capable of further irrational opinions and should be, for that reason, considered dangerous to the community's way of life. Things get so bad that Lenny's wife implores him to cough up the $10 so that they may continue to live with their neighbors in a civil fashion. Lenny agrees, but before doing so he decides that he is going to conduct his own "research" into this.

For the next few weeks, Lenny records each and every train that comes by while he is awake. There are times that he is unable, while he is away from his farm, and during those times he assigns that task to his wife and son. Lenny is not an educated person but he is literate and counting trains is not any harder than counting sheep. He writes down his results and lo and behold, his assertion was correct! There are just as many freight trains as passenger trains.

Feeling vindicated, he shows his results to Jack. Not surprisingly, Jack dismisses his scribbles on a dog-eared notebook accusing him of making up the data, pointing out that there is no way to verify his tallies, that he wasn't there the whole time and that Lenny's wife and son aren't to be trusted anymore than Lenny. Moreover, Ed's data spanned an entire year, yet Lenny only watched the tracks for a few weeks. Lenny retorts that Ed wasn't there the whole time either, he was only present for a fraction of the day, the time in which he waited for a train to pass. Additionally, Ed's data was recorded on paper with pencil just like his. Jack, already biased against Lenny's position and now with *his* money on the line, is unwilling to grant any validity to anything Lenny has to say.

Lenny, empowered by what he has verified in the most scientific way he knows possible, refuses to give in. It is no longer about the ten bucks, it is about integrity and truth. He continues to attend Church on Sundays sitting with his family in an otherwise empty pew. Word of the dispute gets to the pastor who is a fair and reasonably intelligent man, skilled in the ways of diplomacy. He arranges for all interested parties to meet with the pastor himself acting as the mediator. Lenny, offered the opportunity to finally explain himself in front of an audience, is excited about the possibility of clearing his name. Jack begrudgingly agrees.

When the parties convene the pastor is surprised by how many people are in attendance. Lenny and Ed are there with their notebooks, as are Jack and his friends and several other dozen members of the community. The onlookers do not care about the trains, they are wondering how their pastor is going to mete out justice. As each side explains their position it becomes clear that the community members, whose opinion of Lenny has been sullied by hearsay and rumors, side with Jack and Ed. Ed, to his credit, explains that he has nothing to gain in the dispute, he is only there to explain how he arrived at his numbers. The pastor becomes aware that his own credibility is also at stake.

After hearing both sides and examining the notebooks the pastor looks up and summarizes the situation : "Assuming that both Mr. Lenny and Mr. Ed conducted their observations truthfully and recorded their information faithfully we seem to be at an impasse. They clearly point to two different conclusions about the frequency of trains running through this once peaceful town. One of you must be wrong. Jack, it seems to me that you owe this gentleman ten dollars."

Perhaps this may not have come to any surprise to the alert reader. This is a classic error in sampling of discrete events like the arrival of trains. Ed's method, though observing an event in a seemingly random manner temporally is in fact not random. Although he arrived at the tracks at purely random times he waited a varying period until the event (the arrival of a train) occurred. His method *assumed* that there was no relationship between the arrival of freight trains and passenger trains. In fact freight trains and passenger trains were always coming through the town as a pair, the *freight train always scheduled to pass by exactly 10 minutes after the passenger train.* It was five times more likely that Ed would have arrived in the fifty minutes after the freight train passed than the ten minute window after the passenger train. Hence, his data did not accurately represent what was really going on. The best way to get to the answer is to simply hang around the tracks and count trains as they came by; in other words, do exactly what Lenny did.

This hypothetical vignette is demonstrative of several aspects of what is playing out in our society today. First is the tendency of the public to grant validity to what it is being told without a serious examination of the facts or how they were obtained. In this case, nobody really cared enough to cross check Ed's conclusions. It really didn't matter to anyone what the ratio of passenger to freight trains were, so why bother verifying the data? In today's world we may care about events that are transpiring around the world but we have little means to verify them. We implicitly rely on our media sources. As these sources have increasingly veered away from each other we either resign ourselves to be kept in the dark or simply go along with whatever fits into the perspective we have forged over the years. Relying on "intuition" or our own personal experience is neither practical nor easy for a society that has grown accustomed to deferring to others.

Source of Bias #3: Unbalanced inquiry

What might have happened if rather than wager about the truth, Jack and Lenny decided to investigate Ed's results themselves? It would have been far more likely that Jack would have accepted Lenny's careful observations. Perhaps they would have scratched their heads about why the two sets of data were so different. They may have been able to figure out the flaw in Ed's method. If they didn't, Jack would have at least respected Lenny's position. Once there exists a *motive* in being right it is very easy to allow bias to enter our perception. Lenny's method of counting trains was unequivocally correct and sufficient to overturn Ed's results. Jack, however, ignorant of the sampling error in Ed's approach and with his own $10 on the line, became a self-appointed expert in statistics. Jack also goes so far as to assert that the quality of the notebook Lenny has used has some bearing upon the authenticity of the data recorded on it. Unfounded accusations are often leveled against the minority *while the consensus position is not scrutinized to the same degree.*

Source of Bias #4: No capacity to understand the relevance of the information

Although we live in a society that protects the freedom of expression as our very first right as individuals under the Constitution, it is not always easy to exercise it in the face of seemingly overwhelming opposition. Lenny and his family suffered because their community rejected them. For this very reason alone, we should *expect* that minority opinions will not be expressed as freely as those held by the majority. The less the minority feel empowered to voice their concerns the harder it becomes to do so. Public opinion will slowly but surely get less and less accurate the more antimony minorities face. Few in this hypothetical farming town would have felt comfortable supporting Lenny in this dispute because of potential blowback to them.

Perhaps the most salient part of this story has to do with Lenny's conviction to his own sensibilities. As we plod on in our quotidian activities, day after day and year after year we have less and less opportunity or desire to deeply dive into any topic outside the narrow scope of our focus. How can we expect the average person to ever challenge what he is being told by "trusted" or "questionable" sources if we rarely have the capacity to assess the information itself? Lenny was able to stand fast against Jack's conclusion because he was intimately familiar with the subject. We are seldomly given this opportunity and because of that, we may be rapidly losing the ability to think for ourselves.

Source of Bias #5: Overconfidence in an adopted opinion

The story veers from plausibility to fantasy with the introduction of the Pastor. Although we would like to imagine a thoughtful, just, insightful authority appearing as needed to resolve conflict and shine light upon the darker corners of our reality, that person or thing does not exist--outside of ourselves. As long as we hope that another will embody this irreplaceable archetype we may continue to drift about in a current of misconceptions and assumptions. But how could we have expected Lenny or Jack to so eruditely summarize the misguidance of Ed's approach to interpreting this tiny cross section of reality? That IS the challenge. Neither of these two characters would have arrived at a clear picture as long as they were maintaining an accusatory posture. However if they put aside their prejudices and sat by the tracks together for an afternoon it could have placed reality well within their grasp, or at the minimum encouraged them to look into things more deeply.

This hypothetical story demonstrates how bias can quickly develop in the minds of two reasonable people when personal threat or gain hangs in the balance. However there is even a more subtle source of bias that is lurking under the surface. Let us return to the point where the discussion between Jack and Lenny turned personal. This was the moment where Jack and Lenny made a bet. Why did they do it? Clearly they each thought the other was mistaken, but is that the *real* reason? Notice that at the moment that the bet was accepted neither party considered the validity of the other's reasoning nearly as much as their own. Thus it would be more accurate to say they wagered not so much because they believed that the other was wrong as much as they believed that they were *right*. What is the difference and what does it matter?

When you believe your position is unassailable there is little reason to explore how the opposing party came to a different conclusion. This bias arises from overconfidence in an adopted opinion. On the other hand, if you realized that your own conclusion is likely *but not certain* you would be more likely to approach the opposition with curiosity and be less willing to stake anything on your own potentially wrong idea. This is why it is essential to remain aware of the belief that underpins any theory that one holds as true. Recall that our entire scientific model of the universe is based on laws that cannot be explained.

Source of Bias #6: Presumptive legitimacy granted to a source because of personal feelings

When Jack was confronted by Lenny's opposing opinion he didn't give much thought to Lenny's reasoning. Though never counting trains himself, Jack was blind to the fact that Lenny, who watched trains go by his own home every day, had a more intimate perspective than he did. This should have been a warning sign to Jack that would have prompted a reexamination of his position. Why didn't it?

When Lenny challenged Ed's conclusions, Jack didn't see it in exactly the same way. Jack, who had never sat by the tracks for a day, felt he knew the answer because that is what Ed told him. From Jack's point of view, Lenny was challenging more than a conclusion based on an interpretation of data, he was challenging the real foundation of his opinion: *his trust in Ed*. A clear-minded Jack would have been able to separate the idea of Ed's honesty from his ability to design a proper method to estimate the relative occurrence of two types of potentially non-random, discrete events. Lenny was only challenging a conclusion, not the trust between two close friends.

This is exactly what is happening in our world today. Our opinions have become extremely personal because we have decided to equate the devotion to our opinions to the devotion we have in their source. There is no reason to do this. We may venerate our teacher, our friend or our news source but a clear mind will understand that opinions are just opinions; they are ideas that can be cherished now and discarded at a later time. When we brandish our own or attack another's we are acting from emotional attachment and not insight. The greatest respect we can offer an idea or system of thought is an open and thoughtful consideration of it. When we instead accept a belief without a dedicated exploration we are in fact doing a disservice to the belief *and* the source.

Now that we have dissected this story to the core and have explained the source of error in observation and deduction, there is another interesting point to consider. Can you put yourself in Jack's place at the coffee shop when his disagreement with Lenny arose? How would it *feel* to have that level of confidence in your opinion about something? How does it compare to how Lenny might have felt? The difference, if you could imagine one, is one that reflects the difference between believing and *knowing*. Perhaps it is subtle or indistinguishable to you. Perhaps it is palpable. There isn't a "right" way to feel about it--it's purely subjective. However one objective way of comparing the two levels of confidence is to ask yourself this question, how many people would have been able to talk Jack out of his position? We can assume at least one person could have : Ed. If Ed had arrived that morning admitting his approach was flawed or that he had made an arithmetic error Jack would have changed his tune. On the other hand there isn't anyone who would have made Lenny change his mind. Regardless if he was right or wrong it would be fair to say that by this measure Lenny was more confident than Jack. Confidence should not be equated with "correctness", it just happened to turn out that Lenny was right in this particular matter.

Although we may seek to have the kind of confidence Lenny has, we rarely have it. We hold complex narratives about our world that fall outside our narrow scope of personal experience. This may not seem like a problem but if we are truly interested in being objective it is worthwhile to recognize what uncertainty *feels* like, especially when it is subtle.

CHAPTER 2:

Whodunit?

Y ou have been chosen to sit on a jury at a murder trial. The defendant, who claims innocence, is charged with shooting a convenience store clerk and taking $300 in cash. The prosecution knows that in order to get a conviction they must establish that the young man charged with this crime is in fact, the murderer.

The undisputed facts are as follows: A lone bystander witnessed the defendant leaving the premises in a hurry shortly after gunshots were heard. The defendant comes from a disadvantaged family and has been in trouble with the law in the past, being picked up for possession of marijuana twice. Although the young man did not have a gun registered to his name, he has friends who possess or have access to firearms. One of these friends has reluctantly come forward, claiming that the defendant was with him at the time of the murder. The two were at the friends house getting high and playing video games. This is the defendant's sole alibi.

The prosecution's approach is typical. They build their case around the eye-witness who has picked the defendant out of a line-up and then back it up by establishing that the defendant had means and motive. The latter two elements to their case is a more difficult task. How is one to know whether he *would* have and *could* have pulled this off? This is why they spend a large amount of time painting a picture of what this young man's life was like, who his friends are and how much respect for the law he had.

The defense has centered around the testimony of the defendant's alibi. It is true that only one person can vouch for him, but that is no less pertinent than the single witness the prosecution can offer. Furthermore, although he has been in trouble with the law for marijuana possession, he has never been charged with dealing drugs. The marijuana, the defendant claims, was for personal use. Although the defendant is poor and was raised by a single mother there was no history of violence in the home, and the family never owned a gun.

You have been chosen to be a part of this man's jury of peers by the attorneys on both sides because you have a reasonable respect for authority and you appear to have little cultural or social bias. After hearing all of the evidence and cross-examinations you and your fellow jurors convene to discuss this man's fate. During the trial you had been paying very close attention to what was said. You have been weighing each piece of relevant information in your mind, trying, as a first pass, to quantify the validity of what has been presented. You suggest to your peers that the most methodical way of assessing the evidence would be to assign a level of confidence to each piece of evidence and proceed from there. Everyone agrees.

The first and perhaps the most important piece of evidence is the eye-witness. He seemed trustworthy. He had his glasses on. He was perhaps fifty feet away. However you know that eyewitnesses can often be wrong. Though the witness was able to pick the defendant out of a line-up, the court was never shown who was included in the line up. Were they all similar in appearance or were they of different ages and sizes? Everyone weighs in. Not surprisingly everyone has a somewhat different opinion about how much the witness' testimony can be trusted. The average confidence is, let us say 80%. In other words the jury as a whole believes there is an 80% chance that the person the witness saw leaving the store at the time of the murder was in fact the defendant.

Next you examine the validity of the alibi. Is he lying? Possibly. He is a friend of the defendant and would be motivated to cover for him; he isn't an objective bystander like the eye witness. Perhaps he was in on the whole thing. He admitted to doing drugs with the defendant. Why was he so reluctant to come forward? Perhaps *he* was the one who pulled the trigger. The prosecution did a pretty good job of characterizing him as "unsavory". A poll is taken and again, the average is 80%. In other words, the jury, on first pass, concludes that the alibi can only be trusted 20%. There is an 80% chance he is lying to the court.

Finally you address the means and motive. The defendant was not wealthy and could have definitely used the cash. Likewise, he did not have access to a gun but could have easily borrowed one from a number of sources. But would he have actually pulled the trigger and taken another man's life for three hundred dollars? The man liked to smoke pot. He was not shooting heroin. It is unlikely that the defendant would suffer the same intensity of opiate withdrawal that drives an addict to stop at nothing to get his next fix. It becomes a matter of life and death to that kind of person. An element of doubt surrounds this piece of the story, like in all the other parts as well. The jury agrees that there was indeed means and motive and that there was again an 80% chance that there was *enough* means and motive for the defendant to commit the crime, based on each juror's personal feelings about the matter.

Source of Bias #7: Misunderstanding the pertinence of the evidence

So, in summary, you have boiled down the case to three pieces of evidence. In each case, the validity of the evidence is 80% in favor of the prosecution. Everyone must agree that being 80% confident that the defendant is guilty is not enough to convict the defendant of the crime. There is *reasonable* doubt.

The jury exonerates the defendant. You and your fellow jurors decide to go out for lunch together and talk about the case. Everyone feels differently about the outcome but all give credit where credit is due. You are singled out for your clear-minded approach to assimilating the evidence and obtaining consensus. Not surprisingly there is a large variance around how each individual juror describes the situation. A few believe that the evidence was shaky to begin with and that justice was served. Others believe that the defendant got out on a technicality. They happen to have had a 95% confidence in the evidence but had to concede that that still constituted a reasonable doubt. On average the jury as a whole felt that there was an 80% chance that the defendant was guilty. Are they correct?

No they are not. Why? The prosecution had to establish the identity of the perpetrator, motive and means beyond a reasonable doubt. If any *one piece* of their argument was wrong, their hypothesis *in entirety* would be proven wrong. If the defense was right about *any one* of their arguments it would upend the prosecution. In other words, the prosecution had to be right about every piece of evidence, *the defense had to be right about just one.*

Examining the situation from a statistical perspective, what are the chances that the prosecution was actually correct in their argument? In order to identify the killer the witness had to be correct, the alibi had to be lying *and* that there was motive and means. All three pieces of evidence had to be valid. What was the probability that *all* three pieces were true? The answer is straightforward mathematically : it is 0.8 x 0.8 x 0.8 = 0.512, or 51.2%. In other words, based on the jury's own assessment of the evidence there was essentially a 50/50 chance that the defendant was innocent!

Perhaps this fact comes as a surprise to you. If so, you would not be alone. But what difference would that have made in this case? The defendant would have been exonerated either way. Obviously the point here has nothing to do with the outcome, it has to do with another often overlooked origin of bias. Theories in place tend to stay in place longer than necessary because when those who subscribe to the theory dismiss a piece of contrarian evidence they remove it from consideration for ever more. This directly leads to an unfounded level of certainty. But how does this lead to bias?

Source of Bias #8: Confirmation Bias

The jury felt that the eye-witness had a 20% chance of being wrong. This means that when they look at the next piece of evidence they are, at that point, 80% sure the defendant was guilty. They next consider the next piece of evidence, say, motive and means. There is another 80% chance there was enough motive and means for the defendant to kill. Now when they consider the last piece, how certain should they be in the defendant's guilt? The answer is 80% of 80% or 64% (0.8 x 0.8 = 0.64). When they consider the final piece of evidence, the defendant's alibi, they should be only 64%, or less than two-thirds confident in the prosecution's theory. Does their level of confidence play a part *in the manner* in which the final piece is examined?

In our example we had only three pieces of evidence, each with an 80% probability of incriminating the defendant. However let us say there was yet another fact to consider. A young man with a resemblance to the defendant was picked up an hour after the murder buying $300 worth of drugs from a local dealer. The defense claims that *he* instead was the murderer. They have no proof of this, and this other person is not on trial. However if they were right, it would irrevocably exonerate the defendant. Nothing can be known with absolute certainty. You the jury concede that there is a possibility, say 1 in 5, or 20% that the defense is right. The chance that the prosecution has found the killer is now 0.8 x 0.8 x 0.8 x 0.8 = 0.41, or 41%.

It should be clear to see that the more evidence *required to be true* for a theory to be correct, the more likely the theory may be wrong. It may seem natural to think, "Not only is there an 80% chance I am right, there are *three different* pieces of evidence to back it up!" Only the very clear minded would admit that, "I could be wrong about three different facts which means I may as well flip a coin." Bias is introduced into our thinking when we consider, dismiss and move on rather than holding all data points in consideration simultaneously. What has been dismissed should continue to determine our level of confidence as new data gets presented. This is absolutely necessary if we are assessing the validity of any paradigm that carries with it some level of uncertainty.

In this situation let us look honestly at how a juror would regard this new fourth piece of evidence--a different guy buying $300 worth of drugs in the same neighborhood an hour after the murder. If you, a juror, mistakenly believed that there was an 80% certainty that the defendant was guilty there would be an appreciable difference in how seriously you would interpret this new piece of information than if you realized that after the three pieces of evidence you could barely be 50% certain of the identity of the perpetrator.

This type of bias is different from what our train-counting friends suffered in the previous chapter. Jack and Lenny had something to be gained or lost depending on the outcome. In this situation, though earnestly seeking to be objective, you could easily be biased if you assume an unfounded level of confidence in your position. When that confidence erodes the rigor that you apply in assessing the next piece of data, bias enters the picture. This is called *confirmation* bias, a situation where evidence that confirms your suspicion is more readily accepted and evidence that refutes is more readily dismissed. You may be quick to see that confirmation bias gathers momentum as more evidence gets selectively included when in fact the validity of the entire argument is actually being eroded.

This hypothetical situation is offered as a simplified example of how we interpret our model of reality. Many long and widely held narratives are based on various pieces of evidence that each have an element of uncertainty. Though when examined independently they each have a significant probability of being true, when all facts that need to be *necessarily* be true are considered together, the validity of the theory will be less assured than the validity of each separate piece of supporting evidence. Biases are pervasive, numerous and hard to avoid. Later in the book we will explore how they affect commonly held ideas and shape how we see the world and make major decisions.

CHAPTER 3:

Because **WE** say so

"The ignorance of one voter in a democracy impairs the security of all."
—John F. Kennedy

Dictators and despots, princes and popes, tsars and sultans have enforced their will upon the vast majority of human beings on this planet for many centuries. It is only relatively recently that we as a species have experimented with parliaments, representative democracies and various other flavors of "rule by majority". These newer systems of government seem more just than those where the many are subject to the whims of a few or the one. However they have given rise to arguably the most immanent form of bias in the human psyche today. This bias, or unchallenged belief, is the assumption that *the majority will eventually arrive at solutions that serve the greatest number of people.*

Source of Bias #9: Presumptive legitimacy of the Majority

We know that in many democracies the majority of the people, by their own choice, do not vote. There are several reasons for this. There are the cynical who believe that voting will make no difference to them in any meaningful way because they feel that the process itself is rigged towards an unavoidable outcome chosen by a few. Others do not participate because they are too busy just surviving and cannot be bothered by the whole process. The group that demonstrates the type of bias we are examining here are the ones who don't attempt to understand the issues and what is at stake because they feel that there are enough *other* people putting in the effort. They support the axiom that the majority will get it right sooner or later. They choose to support whatever is popular without careful consideration. If you care but you don't know, what is so wrong with going with the flow?

It is reasonable to assume that in most instances the majority will arrive at the clearest understanding of an issue and act accordingly. However this assumption is valid *only if every member of the majority has arrived at the ascendant opinion independently.* What would happen if half of the majority votes 'nay' only because they believe the other half of the majority is doing the required research and coming to that same conclusion? The majority opinion could in fact be formulated by a minority of individuals. This power of a large group of individuals to "know best" gets diluted by those who defer to others. The more people who defer to the majority, the less likely we will collectively "get it right".

To better demonstrate this phenomenon consider the popular game show that has aired for the last twenty years called "Who wants to be a millionaire?". In it the contestant must answer multiple choice questions. Each subsequent question answered correctly allows the contestant to answer another question worth even more in winnings. If the wrong answer is chosen the contestant leaves with nothing. The contestant always has the option of not answering any further questions and leaving the show with the money won to that point.

As a contestant on the show you have available three options for help when you are stumped or unsure of the answer. One of them is the opportunity to "ask the audience". The studio audience is asked to give their opinion, the results are quickly tallied and the results are shown to you. Obviously, you are hoping for a clear majority of opinion. If 90% of the audience believes the answer is "C" you will be much more confident in trusting the audience than if it were evenly divided.

Now let us regard the situation from an audience member. Let us say you were in the audience and were asked to support one of four answers. If you have no idea what the answer is it would clearly benefit the contestant if you simply abstained and let those who are confident in their opinion vote. Sadly that option is not available and you are forced to guess. If most of the people in the audience were like you and had to guess we can assume statistically that the results would be evenly divided among the four answers providing little help to the contestant. However if you were able to briefly communicate with the rest of the audience it may become clear that a large majority was voting a certain way. Would there be any reason to vote differently? No. If you don't know, go with the flow.

On the other hand, let us say that you and most of the other audience members have no idea what the answer is. There are one or two people that claim they "know" the answer. There is no time to ask questions or verify how they came to their conclusions, but they seem convinced. Again, there would be no reason to vote against them; after all you have no idea. Most of the other audience members decide to go along as well. The votes get tallied and once again there is a large majority that reflects the opinion of the one or two "informed" members of the audience. How certain can the contestant be in the results of the survey? Clearly there is a difference between the two situations. Here only one or two people need to be wrong for the whole thing to go badly as opposed to a true majority where everyone weighs in independently. Nonetheless as a voter who is uninformed, there is little reason to dissent in either case.

As a voter, this approach requires less effort and offers a certain amount of security. However this poses an intriguing question: Is there something hardwired in our behavioral patterns that push us towards conformist opinions and away from alternative ones at a *precognitive* level? Is there a tendency to unite that keeps us in "group-think" more than we should be?

In Sapiens, author Yuval Harari offers an explanation for why our species, *Sapiens*, out-fought, out-thought and out-survived all other *Homo* species on the planet. He suggests that it was our unique ability to describe and communicate situations and events that may or may not have had any basis in reality that set us apart from other members of our genus. In other words, we could tell stories and they could not. By uniting under a common idea, story or even myth, thousands (and now thousands of *millions*) of individuals could come together with a shared purpose, identity or belief system to disband our cousins who were, as individuals, more sturdy and just as cunning but not nearly as good at cooperating as we were. Sapiens were able to fight side-by-side with other sapiens because they *trusted* each other for no other reason other than *they believed the same things.*

Trust, Harari proposes, has not only led our species to eventual supremacy over all others but has also allowed us to form communities, governments and global alliances. We can therefore infer that groups with large numbers of dissenters are at a disadvantage when it comes to survival. From this perspective a "herd mentality" confers longevity. Is it possible that as members of the Sapien species we possess and express a herd mentality *trait* that could be undermining the clarity of our decision making because we innately seek to trust each other more than we seek the truth? A group that cooperates may out-compete one that doesn't, however that doesn't mean they are immune to self-destruction. Take a group of lemmings for example. Being great at "Follow the Leader" may be helpful until they find themselves plummeting off of a cliff together.

Source of Bias #10: Repercussions of being the minority

Beyond a lack of curiosity and/or willingness to look harder, what are the other reasons an individual may have to defer to the "majority"? Clearly, conforming to the popular opinion offers a level of security and a sense of shared identity that a minority position does not. Moreover, the more a society vilifies the contrarian, the less likely he/she would be willing to speak out. In the United States we believe we have the luxury of expressing ourselves freely without the fear of reproach or a trip to a gulag. This freedom is, after all, codified in the very first amendment of our Constitution, but is there a *societal* bias against the minority in addition to the bias we carry individually?

Let us take the most extreme example of a generalized contrarian position--what is widely known today as a "conspiracy theory". If you are like most people you will immediately associate a "conspiracy theory" with a twisted, absurd fantasy held by the irrationally paranoid. Given the staggering number of seemingly frivolous accusations directed at widely trusted institutions compounded by mainstream media's unwavering characterization of all conspiracy theorists as unhinged and delusional, this seems like a reasonable reaction. However equating "conspiracy theory" with fantasy before any consideration is, by definition, a bias. Beyond the sheer outlandishness of many conspiracy theories is there another reason, perhaps unseen, that explains why we are biased against them?

Merriam-Webster defines the term *conspiracy theory* as "a theory that explains an event or situation as the result of a secret plan by usually powerful people or groups". The key elements of this definition remain consistent across all authoritative lexicons: the group responsible for an event must be powerful and covert. However, if we refer to the Wikipedia definition as of 11/2018 a new element emerges : "A *conspiracy theory* is an explanation of an event or situation that invokes a conspiracy—generally one involving an illegal or harmful act supposedly carried out by government or other powerful actors—*without credible evidence.*"

When an explanation is labeled a "Conspiracy Theory" it, by today's definition, has no evidence to support it. A theory is an explanation that has supporting evidence. An explanation with no supporting evidence is a *hypothesis*. The term "Conspiracy Theory", as it is used today, is thus an oxymoron. These "Conspiracy Theories" we seem to hear about everyday should really be called "Conspiracy Hypotheses" if there is, by definition, no credible evidence to support them.

Beyond the improper use of the word "theory" what is more concerning is that the "Conspiracy Theory" label identifies an explanation as *inherently* baseless. Though this means that the explanation is not supported by "credible" evidence it is not treated that way in our society. Once labeled a "Conspiracy Theory" it is not considered a possible explanation that may someday be proven. Instead, Conspiracy Theories are relegated to the realm of the outlandish and fantastical. Furthermore, those who believe in a conspiracy theory carry the stigma of being a Conspiracy "Theorist", a label that signifies naiveté or often subversiveness. This is where bias enters the picture. If there were an actual conspiracy afoot today and someone tried to bring light to it, what would prevent that person from being labeled a "Conspiracy Theorist" and not only face the wrath of a society that automatically condemns such people but also be considered to be either the purveyor of false information or embarrassingly gullible? Anyone who came to his defense would also suffer the same fate. How then would a conspiracy ever be revealed? Who decides whether a person is a whistleblower or a conspiracy theorist? We may feel that the facts will eventually "sort themselves out" however there exists, because of the meaning "Conspiracy Theory" now connotes as well as its arguably indiscriminate usage, a very real possibility that an accusation of a *real* conspiracy will be dismissed *prematurely* and never examined again. In chapter 7 we will take a close look at an undeniable example of how the premature use of the conspiracy theory label has quite possibly steered us away from objectivity.

Because conspiracy theories are defined as having no credible facts to support them, what will happen when in the future a piece of evidence arises that is factual and credible that supports the conspiracy in what was previously labeled a conspiracy **theory**? Will this piece of evidence receive objective consideration?

This situation we find ourselves in can be disquieting to some, but for many it is not a matter of concern primarily because of the trust they place in professional media. As long as they can rely on these platforms to diligently give voice to the whistleblower they can feel assured that conspiracies, if and when they are transpiring, will be divulged. Generally speaking, the level of trust placed in these platforms is the most important difference between Conspiracy Theorists and the rest of society. Those of us who believe the professional media is in fact an independent, impartial institution can sleep soundly with the confidence that any "real" conspiracy would be identified before it becomes labeled as a "conspiracy *theory*" and subsequently dismissed. On the other hand, Conspiracy Theorists (as they are called in today's society) are wary of placing such trust in the media. They toss and turn at night because, in their view, by trusting professional media we are being led by an institution that may seem earnest at the surface but at its foundation is irredeemably corrupt. To them the media is a potent tool of conspirators themselves because the media ultimately dictates what is a conspiracy and what is a "conspiracy theory". Interestingly, each side regards the other as astonishingly naive.

Source of Bias #11 : Using the credibility of a conclusion to assign credibility of the evidence that supports it

Most people believe that conspiracy theories have no evidence to support them and that is why they are called conspiracy theories. This may not be true. First, the original definition of a conspiracy theory given above makes no mention of evidence. A conspiracy theory is merely an explanation that involves powerful conspirators acting covertly. However the term has evolved in our vernacular to imply that they are untrue because there is no evidence to support them. The reality is that there might be evidence to support a conspiracy theory, but there is no *credible* evidence to support it. What possible difference would that make? Why even include the word credible when talking about evidence? What would be the point in having *in*credible evidence?

Legally, evidence that is *credible* is that which a *reasonable* person would consider to be true in light of the surrounding circumstances. Can you see the potential problem here? If evidence supports an explanation that seems at the surface to be unreasonable, how does a reasonable person avoid automatically labeling the *evidence* not credible? We are now using the credibility of the *conclusion* to determine the credibility of the *evidence* that supports it. Is this really so important?

Perhaps you are quick to see that with this approach, our understanding of what is true and real can never evolve quickly. If any evidence, *no matter how valid,* arose that unequivocally destroyed our faith in trusted institutions or radically changed our view of long-held beliefs a reasonable person would automatically discard it as "not credible" and remain entrenched in their accepted paradigm. This is the source of the insidious bias that is generated by labeling something a "Conspiracy Theory". *"Credible" evidence cannot be a necessary requirement of a theory that challenges what is credible to begin with.* If you cannot believe the conclusion you won't be able to believe the evidence that proves or even supports it.

For example, let us say there has been a fire at a warehouse. It burned completely to the ground. There were no security cameras. The forensic experts show up the next day and start examining the scene. They find a spot that seems like the origin of the fire but there are no chemical residues of an accelerant or evidence of faulty wiring. Someone shows up claiming they know who the arsonist was. They show the police a picture that they took the night of the fire. In it is a large, green, ferocious looking reptile that clearly seems to be shooting fire out of its nostrils. The "dragon", the witness says, flew away a few minutes later. Obviously the police will assume the picture to be a photoshopped image or just a picture of someone in an elaborate costume. Even if experts claim that the image appeared authentic we can expect that the authorities will assume that there must be a different explanation before putting down "Dragon Attack" on their report even if they do not have an alternative explanation. At this point we can guess that the person who offered the photo will likely be suspected of involvement and the cause of the fire be deemed unknown. Because the existence of dragons is not credible, any evidence that supports their existence is automatically deemed not credible. This is the nature of the bias we are talking about here.

But why is this a bias if we **know** dragons don't exist? The answer is that we don't know that they don't. We **believe** that they don't because there is no proof of their existence--*other than a picture of one burning down a warehouse*! Thus logic and reason serve us up to the point where we are grappling with the seemingly impossible. If an explanation challenges what is credible, what kind of evidence will ever suffice? This is arguably the most pervasive form of bias when it comes to paradigm shifts. How will we ever come to accept the existence of dragons if they indeed existed? You would have to see one for yourself, perhaps several times before believing it yourself. Let's say you caught a dragon on camera. Pretty strong evidence in a courtroom, right? Yet how far would it go in your effort to convince the world that dragons exist? Not very. Your two-minute video would be considered not-credible *because* it suggests that dragons exist. There might be a small subset of people who consider the video to be undeniable proof of dragons. How could the same piece of evidence suffice for them but not the rest of the world? Answer: it has nothing to do with the evidence, it has to do with the credibility of dragons in the minds of those considering the evidence. Evidence has now become subjective. We are either for or against believing the evidence depending on how we feel about what the evidence itself suggests. This is a form of confirmation bias we have with explanations that invoke a conspiracy.

Is this all just hypothetical or have we had evidence of such "dragons" in our history that remained invisible in plain sight because we just couldn't wrap our heads around such things for a very long time? Absolutely. The curvature of the Earth's surface is an example of such a dragon. Humans have observed the moon and its phases for thousands of years. It was obvious that the moon was not flat. Nature offers us the explanation for the crescent shaped moon whenever sunlight falls upon a bunch of grapes. The moon isn't circular, it is *spherical*. Why would we think until very recently that the moon was a ball but the Earth flat? Well, that's what we did. For a very long time. Perhaps we can excuse our ancestors because they needed *direct* proof. Was there any such proof available back then? Yes there was. When we began exploring the seas we clearly saw that as ships moved from shore they didn't disappear all at once. The bottom of the ship vanished before the sails did. Likewise on the ship it was easier to spot land from atop the mast than on the deck. Why would this be the case if the ocean was perfectly flat? There can be no other explanation for this widespread and reproducible phenomenon other than the fact that the surface of the Earth was curved too.

Note that the evidence for a spherical Earth was *valid but not credible*. Despite the overwhelming evidence right in front of our eyes it wasn't until a human being circumnavigated the planet in 1522 that Europeans began to widely accept that we lived on a spherical planet and not a flat plate with edges to be avoided at all costs. Only then could we retrospectively determine that the evidence had been valid all along. Even today there are people who believe the Earth is flat. These so-called Flat Earthers believe they are acting rationally when they dismiss evidence of a spherical Earth because to them the idea that the ground upon which they stand could be curved is impossible. They think everyone else is nuts for believing in dragons. The human mind can be quite facile and adaptive when it comes to making small adjustments quickly. Accepting truths that lead to big jumps in understanding is entirely different for us. In later chapters we will take a close look at a few "dragons" that may or may not be popping up in our world today.

To summarize, there exists a bias favoring an ascendant or popular opinion. This bias can remain in place for several reasons :

- Although an opinion held by the majority is more likely to be true than one held by the minority, we may not be accurately identifying the majority opinion. If a person is not interested in diligently investigating an issue, it is wiser to adopt the majority view because there are more people that have arrived at that position. The more people that adopt the majority view without independently considering it, the more the power the majority has in being accurate gets diluted.
- There is a possibility that conforming to the popular position is an innate tendency of our species.
- There exists, even in a society that protects the freedom to express independent opinions, the risk of personal attack from the majority if one chooses to express a dissenting opinion.
- If the independent, contrarian or minority opinion specifically challenges the integrity of trusted institutions such as the government or the media it runs the risk of prematurely being labeled a "Conspiracy Theory", a term that signifies baselessness. Because these explanations suggest *conclusions* that are deemed not credible, any *evidence* that supports them will rightly be considered "not credible" as well, even though the evidence may be in fact quite valid. In other words, evidence that suggests a conspiracy is regarded as fakery because the idea of a conspiracy, especially a very large one, is hard to believe to begin with. Furthermore, once an explanation is widely touted as a "Conspiracy Theory" finding a truly objective audience for any *new* evidence becomes much more difficult. Thus the explanation will continue to be considered baseless, perhaps indefinitely.
- Evidence supporting theories that indict the media is ultimately validated or refuted by the media themselves. Though this arrangement does not necessarily mean that the integrity of the media is suspect,

it does leave us open to a potential hijacking of collective opinion by a very powerful institution that may not be beyond reproach.

Can we expect the media to police themselves? Conventional wisdom dictates that this is an acceptable expectation. Obviously there exist large platforms that are not dedicated to diligent research, source checking and objective reporting. These sources are profit driven institutions selling propaganda under the guise of "reporting the news". However there are many others that hold objectivity and dedication to balanced reporting as their primary mission. Tens of thousands of journalists with honorable intent are ostensibly endeavoring to separate fact from fiction, double and triple checking their sources and seeking opinions from experts so that the public can draw their own conclusions. The idea that they could all be in cahoots to cover up a conspiracy or truths that would radically shift our world view is impossible to believe.

However most media platforms, even the most venerated ones, are under the control of a very few people. Do these few wield enough influence to direct their organizations to create narratives that are disingenuous or overtly inaccurate? Considering this possibility may be construed as an insult to all those who dedicate their careers in journalism to conveying truth and holding their colleagues to similar standards. However is it possible that these powerful moguls could direct their organizations away from a very few *specific* narratives, or perhaps just a single one that suggests a solitary but very deep but unlikely conspiracy? Would these powerful individuals ever benefit from hiding big truths from the general public? Note the bigger the conspiracy, *the less credible it is*. The less credible it is, the easier it is to divert eyes from it, especially those of a person trained to be as objective as possible, e.g. a journalist.

At the same time, an explanation involving a particularly large conspiracy is more likely to gain traction in a much smaller group of people who are open to such stories either out of gullibility or because they are easily seduced by the glamor of being in an exclusive group that knows what the "real" truth is. Notice how an authentic whistleblower can easily be thrown into that group by association. Once labeled gullible or a "Conspiracy

Theorist" their stories or proof of a true conspiracy risk being discarded through *ad hominem* attacks. In other words they will be judged on their character and not their opinion on the subject. The only hope they have to distinguish themselves from their cohorts is through legitimacy granted by the media.

We are faced with the unavoidable reality that the media cannot recuse themselves from the picture. They are our only eyes on the world. In this sense we are in a very similar situation that our ancient ancestors were in. How do we know we are seeing the whole picture? Are "Conspiracy Theorists" the curious and sometimes annoying members of the tribe that regale us with fantastical stories by the fire or are some of them in fact the hawks seeing things from above?

As we will examine in the following chapters, "Conspiracy Theories" are nothing new, they have existed in our collective psyche since we have been living together in large, self-governing communities. They can be extremely destructive, especially to societies that are constantly balancing the freedom of expression with the need to maintain trust in authority. However logic dictates that by throwing *every* conspiracy theory into a bucket of reprehensible ideas to be permanently jettisoned for the good of all we may be missing an important signal in the noise. The only way to be sure that this is not happening is to openly examine every such theory on its own merit, but who has the patience, time or resources to do this? This has become the duty of the media, an institution that may have a conflict of interest in the matter.

At this moment, it is useful to simply acknowledge that a society that depends on its "trusted" news sources to sort out theories that question the integrity of authorities or the media itself runs the risk of being hoodwinked sooner or later. How would a society in this situation know if the media is "secretly working with other powerful people or groups" to keep certain crucial facts hidden from public view? In other words, how would we know of a conspiracy that involved the media *itself*? This is a vitally important question to ask of ourselves. If the media were part of a conspiracy how would it be "reported" to us? The answer is that it won't be. We would have to deduce it.

First we would need to acknowledge that our own position, one that is based in our trust in the professional media may not carry the absolute certainty we have assumed. Recall that Jack's steadfast trust in Ed contributed to his inflexibility in seeing the whole picture. Unfortunately, unlike the townspeople in Chapter 1 we do not have a pastor figure to point out our blindspots. We must rely upon our own wits.

We are also placed in a much more difficult position than Lenny was. Lenny had it easy because he was questioning facts that he was intimately familiar with and could verify independently. How can we engage our objectivity if we must rely on third party sources for our "facts"? If we cannot verify information independently, any new insight concerning the integrity of our information sources must come from outside the sources themselves. This is an uncomfortable but inescapable reality that we are facing today and one that we will continue to face in the future whether or not we are truly interested in "seeing" more clearly. The remainder of this book examines this conundrum from historical and current perspectives.

Before moving on it is important to notice another important fact. The number of people who are challenging mainstream media narratives is growing. There are a number of reasons for this. With the internet we have an unprecedented ability to not only access independent opinions but to also voice our own. Our own Commander in Chief has coined the term "Fake News", a means of repudiating the media's integrity that is now coming directly from what has been, until recently, widely considered the most venerated office in the land. This has undoubtedly energized factions of our populace that are prone to believing "unconventional" narratives, whether they are espoused by the President or not.

There is also the possibility, though generally considered slight, that some of these narratives are gaining traction because they are in fact true or truer than what we have been told. As we have examined in this chapter, the relative popularity of an idea is not necessarily a measure of its validity. However what can we observe about the fervor of these "Conspiracy Theorists"? We can safely say that many are passionate about their beliefs. Many behave as if they have seen something that they cannot unsee. This does not validate their position any more than Lenny's confidence validated his, but it does invite the rest of us to take pause. Why are they so insistent that they are right, especially when it exposes them to ridicule and character attacks from the majority? The answer is not as obvious as one might think.

Clearly with the advent of the internet and the free exchange of ideas more people with alternative views are emboldened to express themselves, and we may only now be observing what had been a latent aspect of our population. It could also be due to the fact that more of us are losing our marbles for some unknown reason. There could be another reason. Let us say, hypothetically, that you saw a "dragon" yourself. Being rational, you would doubt your own eyes and continue to believe that they do not exist and shrug your shoulders about your experience. What if over time you have other encounters with dragons, sometimes even in the company of others who corroborate your experience? Even if you and your fellow witnesses report this to your local TV news station it is not going to be aired or even taken seriously. It would be frustrating but now you no longer have any doubt in your mind that dragons exist. What kind of argument or proof would talk you out of your position? There would never be any. No one can ever *prove* that something doesn't exist. We can only prove that things do.

People like you who have seen dragons stand on unshakable ground because they know they will never be talked out of their position through "logical" arguments or any kind of evidence. "Debunkers" may offer alternative explanations to what you observed but their explanations generally have little impact on someone like you who has had a direct experience of a dragon encounter. Instead they more often exert their influence on the attitude of the majority, making them less willing to openly consider your story because now they have been given a way to explain what you experienced without giving up their paradigm. It is important to remember that here we are talking about a hypothetical, unpopular but valid belief, not a myth. Ultimately myths can be debunked. Truths cannot.

Let's examine a hypothetical population and how they feel about a hypothetical "fringe" belief, like the existence of dragons. Most people don't believe in dragons. A tiny few do. If dragons truly are a myth, the popularity of the belief in dragons will grow or shrink as a function of how much there is to gain or lose by believing in such things. If a society offers no incentive or punishment to those who believe a myth we can expect that the popularity of the myth should remain constant over time. On the other hand, what if the fringe belief is actually valid (i.e. dragons are real) but not yet accepted by the vast majority of the population because very few have had any direct experience that would validate the belief? We can expect that the belief will slowly gain in popularity as more people have dragon encounters themselves. After all, if you have seen a dragon with your own eyes there is little chance that someone who has not had your experience will ever talk you out of your belief. Once you have seen a dragon there's no going back.

How then should we regard the *validity* of a belief that continues to grow *despite a large societal bias against it*? Logic indicates that there is a very reasonable possibility that the belief is not a myth at all. Is this what is happening with some conspiracy theories and their undeniable increase in popularity? How objective are we being with some of these "Conspiracy Theorists"? Is it time to spend an afternoon by the train tracks with them?

CHAPTER 4:

The Biggest Conspiracy Theory

"Look up at the stars and not down at your feet. Try to make sense of what you see, and wonder about what makes the universe exist. Be curious."

—Stephen Hawking

T he preceding chapters have pointed out where bias can commonly arise even in the most seemingly objective mind and free society. Personal gain, the risk of a tarnished reputation, confirmation bias and the degradation of majority opinion by too many people who defer to others can all obscure the truth. Furthermore, in this day and age, there is a clear bias against opinions that question the integrity of institutions that bind us together. This bias against so-called "conspiracy theories" may in fact be the modern manifestation of an innate tendency that has offered our species a survival advantage tens of thousands of years ago.

Is this all just hypothetical? To answer this question let us examine an old but very real "conspiracy theory", one that doesn't involve assassinations, mass-shootings or moon landings. Instead, this is one that challenged our ideas about the very ground we walk on.

According to a poll[1] conducted by the National Science Foundation in 2012, if you asked 100 people living in the United States if they thought the sun revolved around the earth you would receive about 25 affirmatives. To most of us, 25 seems like an embarrassingly high number. If you are among the 75% that would have responded oppositely, meaning you believe the Earth in fact orbited the sun, how would you *prove* it to the other 25%?

How do you know you are correct? Simply saying we have pictures from space that prove it is a very weak argument. I would challenge you to then show me a picture from space that demonstrates this incontrovertibly. What kind of picture would you need to prove it to yourself? More importantly, how did we know this to be true 60 years ago, *before* we had any cameras in space? Perhaps you know this is true because you have been taught this or read it in a book. Did the teacher or book explain how we came to this conclusion or was it merely stated as fact? Perhaps you believe this mainly because *most* people believe this, and it would be impossible to fool the majority for so long about something so big. Do you believe this simply because **this is what you have been told**?

The survey results would have been very different relatively recently in our history. Four hundred years ago, over a hundred years *after* Magellan circumnavigated the planet, nearly 100% of Western populations still believed the earth was the center of the Universe. How did this nearly universal view shift so drastically? Even today it is clear that all celestial bodies rise in the East and set in the West. Putting ourselves stationary and everything else in motion seems egocentric given that all motion is relative. Then again, why would this perspective be wrong? I wake up in the same place every day! What would lead me to believe I was the one in constant motion?

Of course, all science textbooks today would place our sun in the middle of our solar system and the earth in the middle of the moon's orbit. If you trusted no one, including textbooks and your grade school teachers, how would you prove it to yourself? If you cannot prove it to yourself how would you be able to prove it to anyone else?

The first observant minds that woke up to the fact that we have a *heliocentric* (sun-centered) solar system that remains relatively motionless against a backdrop of very distant stars were able to deduce it without supercomputers and satellite-based cameras. They did this with patience and keen observations *over time*. It is impossible to look out the window once and know what exactly is going on up there. As history has proven over and over, it is easy to arrive at the wrong conclusion if you only take a glance at something.

First, they measured the position of the sun in the sky at its highest point (the zenith) throughout the year. The zenith of the sun varies by about 47 degrees between the winter and summer solstices (i.e. December 21 and June 21 in the Northern Hemisphere). In order to explain this with a *geocentric* (Earth-centered) model, the sun's path around the earth each day would not just be in one plane. It would have to corkscrew around it over a period of six months from the northernmost orbit to the southernmost and then head back north for the next six months. This would have been obvious to the earliest star gazers. Imposing that helical pattern *did not prove the geocentric model wrong*, it was just a necessary condition for it to be correct. If we assume that the sun in fact moved in that manner the geocentric model still works.

The constellations were known to appear in the night sky at different times of the year. It was clear that the constellations that disappeared from our night sky during one part of the year did not cease to exist, they were in fact alive and well but were hidden behind the daytime sun. So, in a geocentric model the stars all revolved around the earth every day as well but just a tiny bit slower, *one less revolution than the sun does in a year*. This was the only way that the model could explain how they gradually appeared and disappeared as the seasons changed. If we assume that this is what they do, the geocentric model still suffices.

If you looked very closely, the position of some stars in the night sky relative to each other change very, very slightly depending on the season. The reason for this in actuality is because we are looking at the backdrop of stars from two different vantage points about 186 million miles away from each other. This is the diameter of the earth's orbit around the sun. This effect, called stellar parallax, is similar to what you see if you hold your thumb at arm's length and look at it with one eye and then the other. Your thumb will appear in a different position relative to the background depending on which eye you are looking from. Nonetheless, if all of these motions of the stars somehow occurred relative to each other over the course of the year while still revolving around the earth every day, the geocentric model is still valid.

The planets, in a geocentric model, would also revolve around the earth. They seem to move a slight bit with respect to the backdrop of stars each night as well. Interestingly they seem to be moving in one direction, slow down, reverse direction over a period of months and then return to their original direction again. This retrograde motion is due to the different velocities and orbits of the planets around the sun. Some planets catch up to us in our position in our orbit and pass us, the Earth catches up and passes other more slowly moving planets in more distant orbits around the sun. But this would only be true in a heliocentric model. In our earth-centered model we would have to say that that is simply what they do.

So, with all of these observations we still have two models for how our local universe is set up. One requires very complicated motions of the moon, stars, sun and planets with different periods of rotation around the earth with different speeds and directions. The other would be explained by the sun centered on the solar system with the earth and planets revolving around it in relatively constant angular velocity. Both could explain what is observed from Earth.

Is one model more valid than the other? If the only criteria to judge were the relative simplicity of each model we could easily say that one model is significantly more complicated than the other. But does this make it less valid? Occam's Razor, the principle that the correct explanation is often the simplest, is only an observation, not a method of proof. There is no law that dictates that everything has to be simple. The fact that one model is more simple is not proof of its validity. However the model we choose has deeper implications about our relationship with the cosmos.

The man most often credited with being the first to put forth a heliocentric model of the solar system was Aristarcus of Samos, a Greek mathematician who lived around 270 BC. His idea did not change the popular narrative. His only argument was that his model was far simpler and elegant. Though it could explain the complex motions of all of these heavenly bodies in a straightforward way, it did not **prove** the geocentrists wrong. Nevertheless, by using his model, Aristarcus was able to make the first estimations of the relative size of the sun and moon and their distance from the earth.

Astronomers in the years that followed used the sun-centered model of the solar system to make their celestial predictions because it was easier. There would come a time, however, when their methods would become a liability. This brings us to a fascinating point in European history.

During the first few centuries after Aristarcus' time those who espoused these two different models of our solar system co-existed peacefully. What do you suppose happened next? I'll give you a hint : it wasn't the astronomers who hunted down people who disagreed with them and bludgeoned them with their sun-dials.

Why would subscribers to two different belief systems co-exist peacefully in Ancient Greece be at odds a few centuries later? Neither system denigrated those in the other camp. Each system simply offered a different explanation of what we had all been wondering about for thousands of years. The astronomers did not pose any threat to those who chose to believe in the geocentric model. However they became a threat to an *institution* that sought to control how people thought--an institution that did not exist in Ancient Greece but flourished in the Dark ages.

The centralization of power in the Catholic church began in the fourth century when Emperor Constantine converted to Christianity, ostensibly as a strategy to unify the expansive territory under his domain. Citizens of the Roman Empire lived in various climes, spoke different languages and adhered to different customs. Allegiance would have to come from a different source: a common system of beliefs. The magnitude of the church's authority, serving as the sole liaison between imperfect people and a perfect God, was indirectly related to an understanding of our planet and the heavens above. Humanity's role in the universe as the recipient of the one inhabitable spot in the center of God's creation raised the Church to an infallible status. What to do with the pesky astronomers who offered an explanation that not only challenged the Church's model of how heaven and Earth were put together but also banished humanity to a smallish sized planet endlessly circling the sun like several others? The answers are obvious and the details have been sorted out over the centuries.

As has been repeated throughout human history, authority most often responds mercilessly not only when faced with an existential threat but also one that could potentially impose limits on their absolute power. The present day is no different. This may come as no surprise to some. To others, the idea that we, as educated individuals four centuries after the Renaissance, armed with the scientific method and the freedom to speak and worship as we please could ever be overtly or unknowingly be manipulated, is laughable. (If you happen to be of that camp, would you have been able to prove your position to the 25% who still believe the Sun orbits the Earth? Or did you have to defer to a "trusted" source to explain it to you first?)

During the rise of the Catholic doctrine in the fourth century there were still two perfectly valid models of our solar system. The astronomers, who were the tiniest of a minority, quietly continued to study the sky with an unspoken model of a sun-centered solar system while the majority, empowered by the union of church and state, persecuted them out of the fear of losing absolute control over the way people thought. This continued for nearly eleven centuries before an Italian astronomer, Galileo Galilei, pointed his telescope at the planet Jupiter and its moons and with careful observation, was able to easily show that *not everything revolved around the Earth. All you had to do was* **look**. Galileo was eventually brought to "justice" through the inquisition and forced to live out his last years under house arrest because he refused to recant his position on the matter.

Galileo posed the first real threat to the authority of the church because he was the first person to take things a step beyond Aristarcus by providing clear evidence that the Church doctrine was not just inconveniently complicated but clearly incomplete and possibly even *wrong*. Moreover, by using his primitive telescope any uneducated peasant could see it for themselves. One might guess, then, that that was the end of the geocentric model. It was not.

Independent thought has always been and will always be the greatest threat to authority. For many of us who enjoy life in a free society, the idea that a person would be punished for holding a contrarian belief, especially one that can be independently verified, is unthinkable. In Galileo's day, his imprisonment was not only sanctioned by the powers that be, it was likely considered a holy act.

Though we may be free to believe and speak as we like in this society today, independent thought is only a seed. In the right environment the seed may grow into a mighty tree whose roots can shatter the deepest of foundations. However, in order to grow, a seed of independent thought requires proper soil: people who are *willing to look a little closer.* If members of a society are not curious, even the most brilliant new idea will never be transformative. The idea will remain in the mind of the contrarian condemned to house-arrest. In order to be heard someone must be listening.

The absence of curiosity aside, if a society is *unquestioningly trusting* it can obviously be more easily manipulated too. I cannot speak to the level of curiosity amongst the Italian people in the early 17th century. We can be quite confident, however, that the church exacted unyielding control and that control was born of an unquestioningly trusting population. Corporeal punishment, imprisonment and executions were not physically conducted by popes, or cardinals or those who sat in the thrones of papal authority. Instead it was the faithful and devout who carried out what they believed was God's will, which called for corrective measures against heresy.

Who or what is to blame for this systematic suppression of human thought over those centuries? The few who were in the highest positions of authority likely knew Galileo was not only on to something but was bringing attention to uncomfortable truths that were getting increasingly difficult to hide. It was their edicts that justified action against dissenters. Neither can we excuse the "faithful" for their role. Judging them by today's standards, they were deeply biased. They did not examine the basis of heretical arguments any more than their own unwavering belief in what they were told. As we will examine in later chapters, this arrangement may be more prevalent today than we realize, even in institutions that we believe operate outside of bias.

Galileo's "seed" could not be planted. His imprisonment had little to do with that. It took another fifty years for the final breakthrough that validated Aristarcus' model and catapulted Galileo from a heretic to martyrdom, earning him the posthumous title of "Father of the Scientific Method".

What was the breakthrough? Perhaps you have been able to deduce that whatever proof was eventually found must have been outside the realm of observational astronomy. Although Galileo demonstrated that the moons of Jupiter did not orbit the Earth (which was a matter of some inconvenience to the Church--and to Galileo himself eventually), he could not directly disprove the Earth-centrists for reasons outlined earlier. Simply looking at the sky from the surface of the Earth would never enable the observer to refute or prove either model definitively.

The proof came by way of the Law of Universal Gravitation put forth by Sir Isaac Newton in 1686 more than nineteen hundred years after Aristarcus' day and fifty years after Galileo's death. His law described the behavior of the motions of particles in the universe. These motions could be confirmed independently by empirical evidence. Once his *Philosophiæ Naturalis Principia Mathematica* was accepted as the means by which the motion of objects could be predicted, the Church was forced to concede because they could not explain the behavior of their model with his newly accepted law.

A human being traveled to the moon just 360 years after Galileo "discovered" what Aristarcus had shown nearly two millennia before. How many centuries was this journey delayed because an alternative explanation in ancient Greece became a "conspiracy theory" against authority and convention? As tragic as it may seem, it should come as no surprise that Western civilization took nearly two thousand years to avail itself of the truth in front of its face. Several important sources of bias outlined earlier were in play in the Dark Ages and well into the Renaissance when Galileo lived:

- An accepted theory based on several pieces of evidence that each have a possibility of being wrong is instead regarded as a paradigm with too much supporting evidence to be inaccurate: Most people were not aware that the seemingly unassailable model of an Earth-centered universe was based on arbitrary choices about how to interpret what could be observed. *(Source of Bias #7: Misunderstanding the pertinence of the evidence)*
- An incentive for upholding the ascendant position prevents an open investigation of an alternative theory: We can surmise that people

were reluctant to peer through his telescope for several reasons. The idea that his model of the universe was correct would have been so preposterous that even checking would have invited ridicule from the "sane-minded" majority. There would also be the fear that *he was correct*. What if once you put down his telescope you would realize that the ground you stood on was no longer the stable center of God's creation but a spinning rock tumbling around the sun like the other planets? Surely this would have crossed the minds of those who had the opportunity to look for themselves. *(Source of Bias #1 : Something to be gained or lost by the outcome)*

- The risk of destabilizing a broadly trusted institution that serves as a common foundation uniting large groups of people makes individuals less likely to challenge authority or the authority of the majority: The Catholic Church's near absolute control over people was directly threatened by Galileo's proposal. With no logical argument to defend their position, their only choice was to silence him. Galileo held the Chair of Mathematics at Pisa and then later at Padua. He had been an important contributor to the Italian Renaissance before coming forward with his proof. If *he* was put on trial what would motivate anyone else to support him?*(Source of Bias #10: Repercussions of being the minority)*

Galileo is the "Father of the Scientific Method" not because he refused to be swayed by the threat of condemnation or ridicule. He is credited with that title because he approached the evidence with a sincere desire to know the truth. Remaining objective requires one to consider the facts without dismissing them no matter what their veracity would imply. Galileo's dedication to the facts still stands as the best example of what is required to remain free of bias and what potential benefit can be gained by doing so.

Of course all conspiracy theorists are not Galileos. Neither are all conspiracy theories true. However, can we be certain that all of them are *false*? At their very core, all conspiracy theories directly or indirectly point at a central authority acting covertly and simultaneously at the media for either missing it or looking the other way. This continues to seem unimaginable to many people today. In Galileo's time the Church played the role of authority and the disseminator of information. Today we have a government chosen by the people and an explicitly separate and free press to hold their power in check. Many would admit that even a government freely elected by the people makes occasional mistakes and frequently keeps information from the public but it would never do anything intentionally *egregious* to all of its citizens and then hide it. If it did, whistleblowers would come forward and the media would let us know about it. This is why most believe that such a deception could never occur. The idea that your lover could be in bed with your best friend is *inconceivable*--until it isn't.

Before moving on, let us examine this situation from what would have been a unique perspective at the time. Imagine you were living during Galileo's day before there was an accepted theory or law of gravitational attraction. Galileo himself walks into a tavern and engages you in a conversation over a glass of wine and explains his understanding of what he has been observing in the sky. He never reveals his identity or credentials. You happen to be one of the rare individuals that could see through the bias that was rampant in the community and church with regard to a model of the solar system. You are also able to see through any of your own personal bias around attachment to an Earth-centered model. You completely understand that both models of celestial motion are possible but only one can be accurate. There is no irrefutable evidence for either. Neither model has been "proven". How do you decide which model is the correct one?

Clearly the "objective" position is to shrug your shoulders and claim ignorance. What if you were **forced** to bet on one model over another. Which would you put your money on? The point here is not about choosing the "right" model. There is no "right" model based on facts that were available at the time. If there were anything guiding you it would be beyond objectivity because objectivity *requires* you to admit ignorance in this situation. I call that source of guidance, if it exists for you, intuition. Whether it actually exists or not is up to you. If such a thing does exist, it should be clear that it will not flourish in a biased mind. Perhaps intuition does not flourish in a mind at all. Intuition is the *gut feeling* that everyone alludes to, whether or not they have ever had one about anything.

As you ponder this dilemma with wine in hand, another aspect of the situation becomes apparent. For the moment you are not under any pressure from anyone to make one choice over the other. However it is clear that those in power are applying an overwhelming amount of pressure for *other people* to choose one model over the other. Does this affect your perspective? You can suspect the church has something to be gained from enforcing their position on the matter, but that doesn't mean that they are wrong. Neither does Galileo's "soft sell" mean he is right. Does the situation playing out in the community at large have any bearing on how you will bet? Perhaps. I propose that this is also an aspect of "intuition" which stands in opposition to those so called "intuitives" simply urging us to get in touch with ourselves and "follow our hearts". Intuition requires focused attention coupled with an expanded scope of awareness. This is not something we are used to doing.

Using your intuition does not mean throwing objective reasoning out the window and going with what "feels" right. Objectivity is vitally important and absolutely necessary in order to access intuition. Without objectivity you would never be able to realize that you are at a conceptual impasse with regard to this issue. Objectivity is required to pinpoint your biases, if you have any. Without it you would never be able to engage intuition in a way that serves you and your effort to get to the truth. Simply dropping objectivity and going with your gut on everything will more than likely leave you mired in a false understanding of reality. If I had to choose between intuition and objectivity I would choose objectivity hands down. However there is no reason why we can't have access to both. Know what can be known. Identify what cannot be known and then, and only then, feel what can be felt. There may not be anything to "feel" either but why shut the door on that possibility in a situation where you are stuck? Isn't it more rational to take pause and see if this "intuition" thing has something to offer before flipping a coin?

It is admittedly difficult to access your intuition in a hypothetical situation that takes place 400 years ago that requires you to put aside knowledge that you already have. However the next few chapters will challenge you to engage this level of "knowing" as your biases, if you have any, are identified and dismissed as we explore current narratives like this one that are based on multiple pieces of evidence that each have varying degrees of certainty and significance. In every case you will have to decide where to place your money. As we dissect these narratives you will more than likely realize that there is no "right" answer to any of these questions, yet based on our actions we have collectively chosen a path by default.

As you dive headlong into the rest of the book it is worthwhile to notice one of the most important sources of bias that will arise in your mind as you absorb what will be offered. This is *Source of Bias #2 : Unwillingness to look closer.* Because you have chosen to read this far I can assume that you do not have a lack of curiosity. However this bias often enters an objective and curious mind because of the importance we grant to Occam's Razor, the idea that the actual explanation is the simplest. This general principle is in fact quite robust, however *we can easily apply it incorrectly because we do not look closer.*

Before our model of the solar system was universally overturned through the application of the Principle of Gravitational Attraction the simplest explanation of what we observed in the sky was that everything revolved around us. If at the beginning of the seventeenth century you had suggested that the Sun, stars and planets rose in the morning and set in the evening because the Earth was *spinning* you would have been laughed out of the tavern like Galileo would have been. The Earth revolves around the Sun like the other planets but the moon doesn't? Why concoct such complexities to explain something so simple and obvious to everyone? Beyond the threat of excommunication the problem is that few looked closely enough at *everything* that could be observed before drawing conclusions. As described at the beginning of this chapter, our observations of the relative motion of celestial bodies could be explained by a model that put the Earth in the center of creation but it would require a far more complicated system. Occam's Razor would have given us the right answer but only if we sought to explain all our observations, not just some of them.

CHAPTER 5:

Coming To

"When you arise in the morning, think of what a precious privilege it is to be alive - to breathe, to think, to enjoy, to love."

—Marcus Aurelius

G alileo's struggle to convince the world that our model of the solar system had been misconceived demonstrates how individual and societal bias, both insidious and overt, can keep us locked in a paradigm for a tragically long time. Galileo presented his ideas at the beginning of the 17th century, near the end of the renaissance. For two centuries prior to his contributions, western civilization had been making large steps to emerge from a thousand year period of intellectual stagnancy we aptly refer to as the "Dark Ages." During those centuries of subsistence living under a feudal system and ruthless papal authority over thought and expression, philosophers and intellectuals flourished in other parts of the world. One may say that Western Civilization learned its lesson as Europe finally "woke" and began to embrace and protect scientific ideas and explorations which eventually gave rise to the industrial revolution. Just two hundred years later Europe was enjoying the rewards of military and economic supremacy on a global scale.

Modern society, generally speaking, has solidly and permanently embraced science not only because of its direct contributions to our quality of life but also because it has taught us to be wary of belief systems that cannot be proven. It was objectivity that liberated European civilization from the stranglehold of fanaticism and fear borne of religious fervor. The possibility of another Dark Age around the corner seems laughable today. Making that claim could even be construed as an insult to our emancipator. Science and the scientific method will never fail us.

However before becoming too complacent with our technologies, academic institutions and "irrevocable" individual freedoms, how do we know that we are not in a 21st century version of a dark age at this moment? It is true that much has been learned and accomplished in the last century alone but the same could be said about the beginning of the Dark ages in Europe one thousand five hundred years ago. The contributions of the Greek and Roman civilizations were only a few generations old when Europe plunged into the depths of intellectual stagnation.

We have internet, hand-held supercomputers that can access the entire sum of our species' accumulated knowledge, make phone calls and take crystal clear video. We have planes that can shuttle a person across a continent in a few hours. There is no contesting that life is much different today than it was for a person living in the year 500 AD.

On the other hand, a commoner would have spent their lives laboring for the noble class, struggling to feed themselves and their children while hoping to escape the ravages of famine and pestilence. How many people today live in similar circumstances? Does everyone have access to healthy food and clean water? Does everyone have ample leisure time to enjoy their lives or are they perpetually laboring under crushing debt unable to save for their future? How confident are we that an injury or health issue will not impact our ability to provide and survive? Aside from our gadgets and an elongated life expectancy, how different are the conditions for most people on this planet compared to our predecessors who lived in the Dark Ages? These are worthwhile questions because it is unlikely that peasants living in Europe fifteen hundred years ago would have been able to see the possibility or potential for a different kind of existence. How do we know that we aren't in the same position today? Beyond our complacency, what else is preventing us from living out our greatest potential? The remainder of the book is dedicated to openly considering this question.

In this chapter we will examine the first of several widely held paradigms that could be overtly and insidiously blocking our growth as individuals and as a species. The idea that the Earth was the center of the universe was a seemingly unshakeable belief that eventually fell. Now let us examine another paradigm that is rampant in our world today--one that is literally a matter of life and death. This one involves our very understanding of what it means to be awake and aware and what it means to die. What does science have to offer regarding this topic?

The Mystery of Anesthesia

In 1846 a dentist named William T.G. Morton used ether to allow Dr. Henry J. Bigelow to partially remove a tumor from the neck of a 24 year old patient safely with no outward signs of pain. The surgery took place at Massachusetts General Hospital in front of dozens of physicians. When the patient regained consciousness with no recollection of the event it is said that many of the surgeons in attendance, their careers spent hardening themselves to the agonizing screams of their patients while operating without modern anesthesia, wept openly after witnessing this feat. At the time no one knew how ether worked. *We still don't.* Over the last 174 years dozens of different anesthetic gases have been developed and they all have three basic things in common: they are inhaled, they are all very, very tiny molecules by biological standards and... we don't know how any of them work.

If you closely consider how our bodies do what they do (move, breathe, grow, pee, reproduce, etc.) the answers may be astounding. It is obvious that the energy required to power biological systems comes from food and air. But how do they use them to do everything? How does it all get coordinated?

These are the fundamental questions that have been asked for millennia, by ancient medicine men to modern pharmaceutical companies. It turns out that the answers are different depending on what sort of perspective and tools we begin with. In the West, our predecessors in medicine were anatomists. Armed with scalpels, the human form was first subdivided into organ systems. Our knives and eyes improved with the development of microtomes and microscopes giving rise to the field of Histology (the study of tissue). Our path of relentless deconstruction eventually gave rise to Molecular Biology and Biochemistry.

This is where Western medicine stands today. We define "understanding" as a complete description of how the very molecules that comprise our bodies interact with one another. This method and model has served us well. We have designed powerful antibiotics, identified neurotransmitters and mapped our own genome. Why then have we not been able to figure out how a gas like ether works? The answer is two-fold.

First, although we have been able to demonstrate some of the biological processes and structures that are altered by an inhaled anesthetic gas, we cannot pinpoint which ones are responsible for altering levels of awareness because inhaled anesthetic agents affect *so many seemingly unrelated things at the same time*. It is impossible to identify which are directly related to the "awake" state. It is also entirely possible that all of them are, and if that were the case consciousness would be the single most complex function attributed to a living organism by a very large margin.

The second difficulty we have is even more unwieldy and requires some contemplation. As explained above, western medicine has not been able to isolate which molecular interaction is responsible for anesthetics' effect on our awareness. It would then be reasonable to approach the puzzle from the opposite end and ask instead, "Where is the source of our awareness in our bodies?" and go from there.

We do know that certain neural pathways in the brain are active in people who are awake, but if we attribute consciousness to those specific pathways then we are necessarily identifying *them* as the "things" that are awake. To find the source of their "awakeness" we must then look closer at them. With the tools we have and the paradigm we have chosen we will inevitably find more molecules interacting with other molecules. *When you go looking for molecules that is all you will find*. Our paradigm has dictated what the nature of the answer would be if we ever found one. Does it seem plausible to think we will find an "awareness molecule" and attribute our vivid, multisensorial experience to the presence of it? If such a molecule existed how would our deconstructive approach ever explain why *that* molecule was the source of our awareness? Can consciousness ever be represented *materially*?

A more sensible model would be to consider the activity of these structures in the brains of conscious individuals as *evidence* of consciousness, *not the source of it*. It is apparent that unless we expand our search beyond the material plane we are not going to find consciousness nor be able to understand how anesthetic gases work.

The mechanistic nature of our model is well suited to most biological processes. However with regard to consciousness, the model not only lends little understanding of what is happening, it also gives rise to a paradigm that is widely and tightly held but in actuality cannot be applied to the full breadth of human experience. We commonly believe that *a properly functioning physical body is required for us to be aware.* Although this may seem initially incontrovertible, upon closer examination it becomes quite clear that this belief is actually an assumption that has massive implications. To be more precise, how do we know that consciousness does not continue uninterrupted and only animate our physical bodies intermittently rather than the other way around where the body intermittently gives rise to the awake state? At first this hypothesis may seem absurd, irrelevant and unprovable. Putting absurdity and lack of relevance aside, there isn't any scientific proof that our consciousness terminates with the death of our bodies either. We are left with two different paradigms, neither which can be proven by the standards we have available. However the paradigm to which we subscribe is far from irrelevant. Let's now take a closer look at what we can observe when people have a brush with death or actually "die" by our standards. Is nature providing us any hints?

Patients under anesthesia offer a unique look at the question because they are rendered inanimate, unconscious and as close to death as is possible before they are returned to their normal state. Let us first consider how Anesthesiologists measure anesthetic depth in the operating room. They continually measure the amount of agent that is circulating in a patient's system, but as described earlier, there is no measurable "conscious" molecule that can be found. They must assess the behavior of their patients to make that determination. Do they reply to verbal commands? Do they require a tap on the shoulder or a painful stimulus to respond? Do they respond verbally or do they merely shudder or fling an arm into the air? Perhaps they do not even move when the very fibers of their body are literally being dissected.

There are many situations when a person will interact normally for a period of time while under the influence of a sedative with *amnestic* properties and then have absolutely no recollection of that period of time. As far as they know, that period of time never existed. Indeed, this reproducible phenomenon requires a relatively small dose of drug in the benzodiazepine class (e.g. Valium or Xanax). They have no idea that they were lying on an operating room table for 45 minutes talking about their recent vacation while their surgeon performs a minor procedure with local anesthesia on their wrist for example. Sometime later they find themselves in the recovery room when to their profound disbelief they notice a neatly placed surgical dressing on their hand. I have been told many times that a patient had asked that their dressing be removed so that they could see the stitches with their own eyes.

How should we characterize their level of consciousness during the operation? By our own standards they were completely awake. However, because they have no memory of being awake during the experience, they would recount the experience more or less the same way a patient who was rendered completely unresponsive would. This phenomenon is common and easily reproducible. Moreover, it invites us to consider the possibility that *awareness continually exists without interruption but we are not always able to access our experiences retrospectively.*

During some procedures where a surgeon is operating very close to the spinal cord Anesthesiologists will infuse a combination of anesthetic drugs that render the patient unconscious but allow all of the neural pathways between the brain and the body to continue to function normally so that they can be monitored for their integrity. In other words, the physiology required to feel or move remains intact yet the patient apparently has no experience of any stimuli, surgical or otherwise during the operation. How are we to reconcile the fact that we have a patient with a functioning body but has no ability to experience it? *Who exactly is the patient in this situation?*

Near Death Experiences (NDEs)

If we broadened our examination of human experience to consider more extreme situations, another wrinkle appears in the paradigm. There are numerous accounts of people who have experienced periods of awareness whilst their bodies have been rendered insensient by severe trauma. Near Death Experiences (NDEs) are all characterized by lucid awareness that remains continuous during a period of time while outside observers assume the person is unconscious or dead. Often patients who have experienced an NDE in the operating room can accurately recount what was said and done by people attending to them during their state of clinical death. They are able to accurately describe the event from an observer's perspective, often viewing their own body and those around it from above.

Interestingly, people describe their NDEs in a universally positive way. "Survival" was an option that they were free to choose. Death of their body could be clearly seen as a transcending event in their continuing awareness and not as the termination of their existence. Very often the rest of their lives are profoundly transformed by the experience. No longer living with the fear of mortality, life subsequently opens up into a more vibrant and meaningful experience that can be cherished far more deeply than was possible prior to their brush with death. Those who have had an NDE would have no problem adopting the idea that their awareness exists independently of their body, functioning or not. Fear and anxiety would still probably arise in their life from time to time, but it is the rest of us who carry the seemingly inescapable load of a belief system that ties our existence to a body that will perish. How does this belief serve us?

If you believe that your very existence is tied to a functioning body you would surely live your life differently than if you were certain that whoever you were would continue to exist uninjured after the death of your body. If you believed that your existence ended with your death, how would you live? Hoarding things and experiences and maximizing pleasure would be the most logical thing to do. How likely is it that you will be ever completely satisfied if you knew you only had a limited amount of time to live? Many schools of religious thought profess the existence of a transcendent soul, spirit, Christ consciousness or Buddha-nature that lives after the death of the body, but what kind of world are we living in today? Which paradigm are we actually subscribing to?

When the anesthetic gas is eliminated from the body consciousness returns on its own. Waking someone up simply requires enough space and time for it to occur *spontaneously*. There is no reversal agent available to speed the return of consciousness. The time required to emerge from anesthesia is directly related to the amount of time the patient has been exposed to the anesthetic. At some point the patient will open their eyes when a threshold has been crossed. Depending on how long the patient has been anesthetized, complete elimination of the agent from the body may not happen until a long while after the patient has "woke".

By the time the patient arrives in the recovery room, they are safely on a path to their baseline state of awareness. Getting back to a normal state of awareness may take hours or even days. In some cases patients may never get their wits back completely. Neurocognitive testing has demonstrated that repeated exposure to general anesthesia can sometimes have long-lasting or even irreversible effects on the awake state. It may occur for everyone. Perhaps it is a matter of how closely we look.

Is fear keeping us "Anesthetized"?

Interestingly, it is well known that the long term effects of anesthetic exposure are more profound in individuals who have already been demonstrating elements of cognitive decline in their daily life. Indeed, this population of patients require significantly less anesthetic to reach the same depth of unconsciousness during an operation. This poses an intriguing question. Is our understanding of being awake also too simplistic? Is there a continuum of "awakeness" in everyday life just as there is one of unconsciousness when anesthetized? If so, how would we measure it?

Modern psychiatry has been rigorous in defining and categorizing *dysfunction*. Although there has been recent interest in pushing our understanding of what may be interpreted as a "super-functioning" psyche, western systems are still in their infancy with regard to this idea. In eastern schools of thought, however, this concept has been central for centuries.

In some schools of Eastern philosophy the idea of attaining a "super functioning" awake state is seen as something that also occurs spontaneously when intention and practice are oriented correctly. Ancient yogic scriptures specifically describe super abilities, or *Siddhis*, that are attained through dedicated practice. These Siddhis include fantastical abilities like levitation, telekinesis, dematerialization, remote-viewing and others. It is admittedly difficult for the Western mind to accept that a human being could ever do such things. We believe that a truly rational person would never entertain such fanciful ideas.

Being able to fly through the air or move material objects with thought aren't the most potent of abilities available to the true adept in those traditions. In fact, these traditions regard these gifts (if they do exist) as very dangerous because they can easily distract the earnest seeker away from a greater potential. In these schools of thought the most advanced "superpowers" are those that allow a person to remain continuously in a state of joy and *fearlessness,* ideas that we are interestingly much more likely to accept as possible. Are we too quick to assume that it is easier to be fearless than to "teleport" at will? Why would those traditions ascribe the most importance to fearlessness? Perhaps it has to do with the challenge of remaining in that state and the benefits of doing so. Note that if such a state were possible it would clearly be incompatible with the kind of absolute, psychological identification most of us have with our mortal bodies. It may be of no surprise that Eastern medicine also subscribes to an entirely different perspective of the body and uses different tools to examine it.

Fear has served our ancestors well, helping us to avoid snakes and lions, but how much fear is necessary these days? Could *fear* be the barrier that separates us from our highest potential in the awake state just as an anesthetic gas prevents us from waking in the operating room? It is not possible to remain fearless while continuing to identify with a body that is prone to disease and death. Even if one were to drop the *assumption* that the source of our existence is a finite body, how long would it take to be free from the effects of a *lifetime* of fearful thinking before an individual outwardly manifests changes that reflect a shift in this paradigm? Is it possible that by continuing to leave this model unchallenged we never feel what it is like to be truly awake?

Putting fantastical abilities aside, how can we accurately predict what our world would look like if everyone lived joyfully and fearlessly without the desperate need to maximize pleasure and time? We can postulate that it would be better. Science is suggesting that we may be entirely misconceiving who we are. Moreover we have testimony from those who have actually died (by scientific standards) and returned to tell us that we are worrying about the wrong things. Recall that some who have had Near Death Experiences were not simply having a vivid dream borne of random electrical impulses in a brain in the last throes of life; they were able to recount the details of the "failed" resuscitative efforts of those around them. It seems only logical to accept the paradigm that we are more than our bodies and enjoy the individual and societal benefits of this shift. Why are we so reluctant to adopt this perspective? Are we *biased* and if so, *why*?

The Possibility and Implications of Reincarnation

NDEs are not the only "wrinkle" in our paradigm of life and death. NDEs suggest that there could be a small part of us that transcends an event which we all call death, an undeniable terminal event of a physical existence. In that sense, our physical bodies should be more aptly considered a small and temporary part of our real, transcendent nature. If that were the case, where then do "we" go after our bodies die? The answer may not be as faith-based or speculative as you think.

Let us, for a moment, take a step back from religious doctrine and agnosticism. These two perspectives represent a stark contrast in their approach to the question. One proclaims that the answer is unambiguously dictated in associated "scripture". The other insists that the answer can not be known, at least for the moment. Is there *empirical* evidence that points to a different answer? There is not. We are dealing with a potential aspect of reality that transcends materialism, the philosophical doctrine that nothing exists outside matter and its actions upon itself. We may not have empirical evidence, but just as with NDEs, there is an awful lot of *anecdotal* evidence that may not be getting the attention it deserves.

Dr. Ian Stevenson was a physician and professor of psychiatry at the University of Virginia School of Medicine for 50 years. He served as the Chair of Psychiatry for ten of them. He is best known for his research into the study of *reincarnation*. During the course of his career he assiduously compiled over three thousand case studies of individuals who reported living on this planet as a different person prior to their current life. What is fascinating about these cases is that the subjects are not adults that claim they were Pharaohs or Knights that served King Arthur in a "past" life. The subjects are *children* who caught the attention of their families when they were very young. They would insist that they had lived rather average lives before, had families of their own and recalled their previous name, details and location of their previous home and occasionally, the circumstances around their death. Often they would go ignored for some time but their dogged refusal to recant their peculiar tales was a matter of some curiosity to their families. The fascinating part of every case in Stevenson's data is that the child's parents or others familiar with their story eventually stumbled across convincing evidence that the person the child claimed to have "embodied" in a previous life *actually lived and died before their birth*. Dr. Stevenson would attempt to authenticate the child's account through interviews with the surviving members of the family of the deceased person the child claimed to have been. Sometimes extremely specific details of the previous life were confirmed, such as secrets that were kept between their old self and their spouse or physical details of their previous home that would only be known to those who lived there. When the child was "reunited" with the family of the deceased they could identify many of those in their old family, and pick out the imposters that Stevenson had planted to test the specificity of their recall.

Dr. Stevenson was an author of nearly three hundred papers and 14 books on reincarnation. In 1997 he authored a two volume tome of over two thousand pages titled Reincarnation in Biology that documented the stories of a subset of 225 subjects that not only had specific recall of their past identities that matched those of real, deceased individuals but also had birthmarks or physical anomalies that corresponded to the manner of death of their previous "selves". For example, a child who recalled dying from a gunshot wound in a previous life was born with birthmarks that corresponded to the entry and exit wound of the bullet that purportedly killed that person. If accepted, this phenomenon can be considered more indirect evidence suggesting that our consciousness or "energy body" that represents our transcendent nature gives rise to our physical form and not the other way around. This fits nicely with our observations of patients under anesthesia and the incorrect assumptions we make when viewing consciousness as the result of a functioning body.

His work has been criticized by some who felt his approach to validating these accounts were not rigorous and regard his work as biased and unscientific. Others in the scientific community have defended his methodology and conclusions. Internationally recognized physicist Dr. Doris Kuhlmann-Wilsdorf has stated that based on his findings it is reasonable to conclude that there is an overwhelming possibility that reincarnation is in fact occurring. His work has been covered by <u>Scientific American</u>[2] and <u>The Washington Post</u>.[3]

Why would some scientists dismiss his "evidence" and others defend it? This is where we must be very careful in our own analysis. It is very easy to conclude that because someone has taken issue with his methodology we can shrug our shoulders and dismiss all of his findings *en bloc* and move on. If we choose to do that, are we being objective or are we protecting a belief system that we refuse to surrender? It is also just as easy to proclaim there is finally proof of an idea that we hold dear. For the agnostics among us this controversy is more evidence that the answer is beyond our grasp. Is it possible to be objective about this? Perhaps not. We are dealing with anecdotal evidence, not hard physical proof.

The point here is that it is wiser to acknowledge that certainty is clearly out of reach. A more meaningful inquiry is one where we attempt to assess our *uncertainty* about this phenomenon. Let us take one of Dr. Stevenson's more well known cases, that of Swarnlata Mishra who was born in India in 1948. At the age of three she began telling her parents of her previous life as a wife and mother of two in a different town in the same part of India. Her father was curious and accepting of these tales and began to take notes on everything her daughter uttered about her "past life" lived by a woman named Biya Pathak. She recalled that her family owned an automobile which was quite rare at the time. She remembered the name of the doctor that treated her for what proved to be the cause of her death. She was also able to describe the details and relative location of the house in which she lived, as well as odd details like the fact that she had a few gold teeth. When she was ten her story caught the attention of a researcher of paranormal studies in the area, professor Sri H.S. Banerjee who was a colleague of Dr. Stevenson. He was able to locate the family of the girl's previous life using the notes her father had taken and confirmed the details Swarnlata gave of Biya Pathak. Swarnlata's alleged previous family finally came to visit her. The two families did not know each other. She was able to easily identify her family members and detect the imposter that posed as one of her sons. She convinced her husband that she was once married to him by recounting an incident when she discovered he had taken a sum of money from a box that she kept. No other soul was aware of this secret.

What to make of this? If you are certain that this story is true and represents indisputable proof of reincarnation then there is no need to look further. Similarly if you are certain that the case is a hoax your inquiry has come to an end as well. On the other hand if you believe that there is a remote *possibility* that Swarnlata represents a case of a human being that has reincarnated we can take a step further. How would you assess the probability that her story is evidence of reincarnation? You are once again on a jury assessing evidence. Clearly there are many questions that remain unanswered. How do we know the account is accurate? This is a story of two families who were Hindu and may have been biased towards confirming one of their foundational beliefs. Could they have been scheming? The initial notes were taken by the young girl's father, not Dr. Stevenson or his colleague. Did he fabricate some of it to bring notoriety to his family? We cannot know. The question is, how would you quantify the probability that this story serves as proof of reincarnation? 1 in 10? 1 in 50? There is no right answer here. The purpose of this line of inquiry is to examine how multiple pieces of evidence can affect our level of certainty. In the murder trial from chapter 2 there were only three pieces of evidence. Here we have about 3000 that we can assume for the moment carry a similar level of validity.

Our willingness to grant validity to this and similar stories is completely subjective. This is no different than a jury of peers that regard the same evidence differently. Clearly if you believe in reincarnation to begin with there is no problem in accepting this story as compelling proof. You might say that this one case brings 90 or 95% certainty to the issue. On the other hand, if this stands in opposition to one of your deeply held beliefs you would focus on the uncertainties surrounding the account.

Let us say that Ms. Mishra's story barely changes your level of skepticism around reincarnation. Rather than being 80% certain of this evidence like in chapter 2, you feel that this offers much less proof--say 1 in 500, or 0.2%. In other words, after hearing this reported account you are still 99.8% certain that reincarnation is not real. What happens when we have over three thousand such cases that all offer the same level of confidence? In other words, for reincarnation to remain an impossibility *all* 3,000 cases must have been falsified or inaccurate. The answer is straightforward mathematically :

Probability that Reincarnation is a hoax= $(0.998)^{3000}$ =0.00264

If we were comfortable granting each of Dr. Stevenson's cases just a 1 in 500 chance of being authentic proof of reincarnation we end up with an extremely high likelihood, 99.736%, that reincarnation is **real**. Again, there is no right number to plug into the equation, it is completely subjective. We are simply exploring the power of multiple pieces of data that each carry the potential of overturning a paradigm on its own. If the result is unsettling enough for you to come up with a different assessment of each case you are of course free to do so, however you would be succumbing to *Source of Bias #11: Using the credibility of a conclusion to assign credibility of the evidence that supports it.* There is no shame in this. It is unavoidable when we are dealing with paradigms about "dragons".

Will we ever find the Proof we are looking for?

Dr. Stevenson continued to admit that until a mechanism by which reincarnation can be explained could be identified it would remain a matter of speculation. That is a sentiment of a researcher that acknowledges the uncertainty behind his conclusions. Yet it also invites us to ask what sort of mechanism would we be able to identify to explain a phenomenon that transcends materialism. Are we ever going to be able to "prove" that reincarnation is taking place? If not, what are the implications of plodding along *assuming* that it isn't?

The discussion of patients under anesthesia does not prove that our consciousness remains intact and continuous (though inaccessible retrospectively), however it does point out that this matter is far from resolved. Specifically it introduces the inescapable fact that we are not going to find the proof we are looking for in places we are looking for it. Consciousness seems to transcend molecules, the very things we examine when looking for proof. The challenge to arrive at certainty with regard to this question is identical to the one we faced when observing the skies four centuries ago. No matter how earnestly we looked from the surface of the Earth we were never going to be able to definitively *prove* what was actually going on up there. We should have been able to appreciate that at the time. When the proof arrived it did not come from observational astronomy, it came from physics and the theory of gravitational attraction. When we insist on having *physical* proof of something that transcends materialism before dropping our accepted paradigm about life and death we run the risk of once again being left in the dark for a long while, maybe for *ages*.

What are we to make of the results of Dr. Stevenson's lifetime of investigation? Reincarnation, if it were happening, further supports the theory that death is not "the end". More importantly it should give us another reason to pause. Not only would it force us to reconsider our understanding of death, it also invites us to once again reassess how we should be *living*. Would we change our behavior if we knew we were coming back to this planet for another go at it? What kind of choices would we make if we knew we would suffer the consequences or enjoy the benefits of our decisions made today in another lifetime? What kinds of decisions would we make *collectively* if we all subscribed to the idea that our actions in this lifetime were tied to the fate of our planet and species long after we "perished"? Given the fact that there is uncertainty surrounding this possible phenomenon, is it wiser to assume that he is wrong or right?

Are we biased?

We are now considering a real dilemma, not one based in hypotheticals or history where "the truth" has been dictated to us or revealed over the years. We basically have two paradigms to choose from. On the one hand there is no proof that our existence *doesn't* continue after the death of our bodies. There also is ample indirect evidence that there is more to this life than this material body. We have the accounts of hundreds of people who have died, by our own standards of death, and returned to tell us we have been wrong about the whole thing. Furthermore the idea that there are others who have died and have been reborn on this planet may not just be a fringe belief or part of Eastern religious doctrines. The evidence, if we were to accept it as such, is not being proclaimed by religious leaders or established scientific institutions. It's coming "from the mouths of babes" from all over the world.

On the other hand, we are living in a world where just about everybody behaves in a manner that supports the belief that we each have a limited and finite existence. Simply ascribing *Source of Bias #9 (Presumed legitimacy of the Majority)* or *Source of Bias #10 (Repercussions of being the minority)* to the situation would be short-sighted. It is true that many humans believe in an after-life, or at least profess that they do, however that is not the way *they behave*. The point here is that even if you do believe you are a "transcendent" being, how feasible is it to act in that manner while interacting with a society full of people who are trying to out maneuver you for a bigger piece of the pie? From a purely practical standpoint it is more sensible to play their game and protect and maximize what you have today so that you won't be left with little tomorrow. In this sense, we really don't have much of a choice in the matter as individuals. We are instead being *pressured* to assume a competitive posture because of our collective behavior as a society and a species.

Bias, if it does exist in our minds, will emerge when we instead answer the question, "Are we as individuals and a society exaggerating a self-serving and fear-based narrative?". This line of inquiry leads us to assess the nature of the information we receive on a regular basis. Are we commonly exposed to stories of cooperation, moderation and tolerance? Or are we more often exposed to tragedy, fear and the stories of those whose successes are measured in wealth, fame and youthfulness? How does our media characterize those who eschew the pursuit of material things for internal balance and harmony? Granted the Dalai Lama, for example, has been given international recognition and popularity for this kind of attitude, but how does that compare to the attention we give to people who have outwitted their fellow human beings and ended up with more?

Before we indict the media and the entertainment industry we would be better served by asking ourselves why we are more interested in these narratives to begin with. After all, if we weren't intrigued by these kinds of stories there would be little incentive for them to create content along these lines. I contend that our fascination with this kind of entertainment and news is inextricably tied to our level of understanding of the nature of who we *really* are. More importantly, the stories we are drawn to reinforce the belief that we have only one shot at happiness and a "winner take all" attitude is not just excusable but necessary. In this sense the adversarial relationship we have with each other as individuals or societies gets perpetuated and simultaneously attributed to immutable "human nature". Is this truly our *nature* or are we missing something very big about ourselves? Moreover, are we constructing this idea of reality ourselves or are we being "nurtured" into doing so? Are we forcibly but insidiously being kept in a different kind of Dark Age? If so, what would be the motive in constructing that kind of reality and who would benefit from this? These are the questions the following chapters will seek to address.

CHAPTER 6:

Show me the money

"To be yourself in a world that is constantly trying to make you something else is the greatest accomplishment."

—Ralph Waldo Emerson

W hen you deposit money in a bank, say in a savings account, you have immediate access to that money at any time. Let's say you put in a million dollars. As long as you don't withdraw any money your account balance will always be $1,000,000 no matter when or how many times you check. Yet the bank also serves as a lending institution, presumably using your money to finance mortgages, personal and car loans, etc. We generally believe that the bank is using deposits to finance its lending business. Banks may have millions of depositors and borrowers. For the purposes of this simple example, let us say that you are the only depositor and there is only one borrower. A few days after you deposit your million dollars the bank makes a loan to someone else, the borrower, for a million dollars. What happens when you check your balance? It will indicate that your money has not gone anywhere, yet the person getting the loan has access to a million dollars as well. In fact, let's say he used it to buy a house and that million dollars is now in the hands of the person who sold the house to him. So that person now has a million dollars, but so do you. Where did the extra million come from?

Some may be quick to say that the million has come from other depositors, but that is not true because even if there were other depositors they too will have an unchanged balance in their accounts as well. You may think that it has come from money that the bank has in its "vault", owned solely by the bank itself. But if that were true the bank would have no incentive to act as a savings institution, paying interest on deposits. So where did the money come from?

Getting to the answer to this simple question requires an open inquiry into the banking industry, regulation of monetary supply and the history of the monetary system itself. Though these concepts may seem dry and prosaic at the surface, they dictate how modern society functions and ultimately how we make the biggest choices in our individual lives: where and how we live, what we do with our time, etc. Having enough money is a challenge that all but a tiny minority deal with on a daily basis. Indeed, this topic colors our life more than any other. As we delve into this intriguing mystery we shall see that our commonly held beliefs about the economy and *prosperity itself* could be based on massive misconceptions.

The story of Colonia

Once again let us dive into the hypothetical to get a better understanding of reality. Imagine a large island nation, let's call it Colonia, that exists in complete physical and economic isolation. The citizens of Colonia have diverse occupations and together are able to provide for all the country's needs without the need for trade. They have long ago abandoned a barter system and now rely on currency to manage the exchange of goods and services between each other. The unit of currency is a small but beautiful seashell that used to be buried deep in the sands just offshore. They call this shell the "dollar". All the dollars in the sands around the island nation have been dug up centuries before, and the nation's economy is now based on a large but finite number of these "dollars".

A). The Supply of Money does not limit the size of an Economy

Right away we have our first idea to ponder. Can an economy grow if there is a limited supply of money? Before we can answer this question we must first have a better understanding of what economic growth really is. In basic terms, economic growth is the change in the value of goods and services produced by a society over a period of time. In contrast, a society's wealth is the value of all the things in a society's possession. In that sense, an economy represents the dynamic element of a society, its ability to create value using its labor and resources.

It should be clear that the number of shells in Colonia does not limit how much is being produced. The citizens of the country will work, innovate and produce as necessary to meet their needs whether there are a billion shells in existence or just a hundred. These things will be manufactured, purchased and sold using the country's supply of dollars, regardless of how large that supply is. However the value of what is being produced, *measured in shells,* is inextricably linked to the number of shells that exist. For example, if an ancient Colonia's entire population was just 1000 and they grew a 100 tons of food and built 10 houses and had a billion dollar shells to use to represent these items the value of the food and houses *measured in shells* would be a lot different than if there were only a thousand shells in existence. If a population of a thousand were using a billion shells the average wealth of a citizen would be a million shells. The cost of a house in this case would be "higher" than if the average wealth of a citizen were a thousand shells. Hence, when we add up the value of what the country is producing measured in shells we get entirely different numbers depending on how many shells there are.

A much bigger, modern Colonia with a million citizens would produce much more in the same period of time, however if they were using a fewer number of shells than the smaller version of the country, the value of what is being produced could very well be the same *when measured in shells.* You can see that using the currency as the measuring stick of an economy can also be problematic if the population changes over time.

If we instead measure the size of an economy by the amount of stuff it produces—say the number of homes and the amount of food, the economy will undoubtedly be larger if more people are in the population. The output of an ancient Colonia with a thousand citizens will be much different than of a modern Colonia with ten million in its population even though the number of dollars that *represent* all the country's goods and services might be the same.

We now have arrived at a basic understanding of what money really is. Money serves two interrelated purposes. The first is as a placeholder for value. This is how we normally regard the money in our pockets and bank accounts. Money has no intrinsic value in and of itself, but it can be endowed with value by every individual who participates in a system of exchange. Once the system has been universally accepted, money can then serve as an efficient system for commerce as it does in our own world today. In the possession of participating individuals, money carries a very real value, equal to the amount of goods or services that can be purchased with it. In other words, money only has value if there exists an economy that uses it. What would be the value of all the dollar shells in Colonia if you were the only person living there?

A second function of money is to serve as a means of *measuring* value so that things can be exchanged between members of a society equitably. In that sense money is an excellent means to measure the relative value of items and services at *a given moment in time*. Using it to track the value of anything, from a milkshake to the output of a country *over a period of time* can lead to inaccuracies. It should be noted that the standard approach we have adopted to measuring an economy's size in our world today is to add up how much money was spent over a period of time by all participants in the society. We shall soon see that this may be very well leading to fundamental misconceptions about our prosperity.

B). The supply of money determines Prices

As the population of Colonia has grown what can we say has happened to the average wealth of a person in the country? It should be clear that the per capita wealth must have decreased. For example, if there are say 1,000 dollars in the economy and a 100 people in the country the average wealth of a person would be 1000 dollars/100 people or 10 dollars per person. If after some time the population doubled, the average wealth would be halved (5 dollars). With no more dollars available there can be no other outcome.

This does not pose a problem for the "Colonials" because prices of things will also shift accordingly. As more things are produced, bought and sold the prices of these things must go down. Without any more dollars in circulation how could they do otherwise? There aren't enough dollars in people's hands to maintain the same prices.

This is an extremely important and perhaps puzzling concept to grasp. Holding all other factors constant, *the average price of goods and services is a function of the amount of money in the economy.* Of course the *relative* price of things may change based on shifting demand, supply, or new innovation that results in cheaper production, etc., but the sum of the value of all these things is tied to the amount of currency the country is using. The prices of things are tied to the total wealth of the consumers. The total wealth of all consumers is tied to the supply of money they are using. Note that although the average "wealth" of an individual (measured in dollars) will drop as the population expands and the supply of shells is distributed over a larger population they will still be able to purchase just as much as they did before because prices will have also dropped. We can thus say that *prosperity* has not changed. The value of a dollar, measured as its buying power, however, will have *risen* as more things have been produced by the nation.

These statements hold true as long as the average need of the citizens have not changed. If Colonia gets hit with a hurricane that levels most of the houses, the people will work much harder to rebuild. The value of what is produced during that time will be much higher. Here we are introducing a very important point: if left to themselves, people naturally produce as much as they need.

C). The size of an Economy is best reflected by the number and size of transactions taking place

Let us say that the people of Colonia wish to embark on a large, publicly funded project to build a wall along its entire coast. This project will require one tenth of the country's wealth. Everyone willingly chips in one tenth of their net worth into a public fund and construction begins. What happens to the average wealth of a citizen of Colonia? It goes down by 10% of course. But what happens to prices? They must necessarily adjust to the decrease in spending power of its citizens. Though everyone has fewer dollars under their mattresses no one suffers because they can still afford the same standard of living as before, once prices adjust.

When the money in the "Wall" fund gets spent, the dollars reenter circulation and end up first in the hands of the masons, bricklayers, shovel makers and cement mixers who spend their greater earnings in the market. Prices will eventually re-equilibrate. Although some Colonia citizens directly benefited from this public expenditure, many did not. They still have 10% less money to their name. However, because no money entered or left the economy the prices of all goods taken together will eventually return to where they were. Once again, the value of all things and savings in Colonia combined will be reflected by the total money supply just as asserted previously.

It is worthwhile to pause and reflect upon what just happened. The country has a new wall that cost a lot of money but the total wealth of the citizens has remained constant. Some people have more money than before and others have less, but the per capita wealth has not changed. The citizens have a new wall but the average citizen cannot afford more than they did before. Their prosperity has not changed.

We can easily extrapolate that publicly funded projects can continue, one after the other, adding bridges, universities, infrastructure, etc. by using the same number of dollar shells in existence. This is a fascinating point about an economy in isolation. It can be considered a closed system in that money never leaves or enters it; it merely circulates between purchaser and seller and back again. That being said, a proper measure of an economy's "size" is more accurately a function of its activity. This is why economists measure an economy by the value of stuff that is purchased by a population in a given period of time. When the funds for the wall were spent it resulted in a big bump in the size of Colonia's economy. The average citizen, with respect to their ability to provide for themselves and their families is no better off. This was not unexpected by the Colonials. After all, they willingly sacrificed for a project that would benefit the public at large. The interesting point is that despite contributing a sizable portion of their personal wealth they (as a whole) are no *worse* off either. The country has a new wall, the citizens are holding their own and Colonia's economists can rightly claim that their economy has grown during this period. Notably this was accomplished independent of how many shells were in existence to begin with. These are important points to keep in mind as we further dissect our concept of money and prosperity.

D). Adding or Removing money has no bearing on Prosperity

Now let us say that a diplomat from a foreign nation, Greenspan, visits Colonia and falls in love with the country and its people. He offers to fund the construction of a brand new governmental building complex that will, just like the wall, cost 10% of the total money supply of Colonia. His home country also uses the exact same dollar shells as their currency. As an act of goodwill, his country donates the money. It is hopefully clear that with the addition of dollars into the economy prices of goods and services will necessarily increase correspondingly because more dollars will end up in the hands of consumers. With more money in their hands, they will be willing to pay a higher price for goods and services.

What can we say about the wealth of the country? The per capita wealth measured in dollars will have increased, but the buying power, or prosperity of its citizens will not change in the long run. Aside from the new building complex the people of the country are not any better off with regard to their personal financial situation. They have more shells, but everything costs more too. If the Colonials funded the complex themselves prices would have initially dropped and then returned to their original levels just like what happened with the wall. If Greenspan *leant* the money to Colonia, prices of things would have initially risen but then fallen again to their original levels once the money was repaid and the dollars left the economy. The result of a loan to Colonia is assessed in greater detail in this section but for now let us stick to an exploration of how a changing money supply affects the prosperity of a population.

The rising and falling of prices, which we term inflation and deflation respectively, is actually the result of a money supply that is fluctuating. When money is added through public expenditures, prices will necessarily rise. When money leaves the system, prices must fall. It is therefore more apt to regard inflation and deflation as the *result* of monetary expansion and contraction respectively rather than a phenomenon that arises independently. Of course many factors contribute to the relative price of *individual* items but when we are talking about inflation or deflation we are examining prices of many or all things. Taken as a whole, the value of things measured in dollars is inextricably tied to the number of dollars that exist.

Now we have arrived at an apparent paradox. As described above, it doesn't matter whether the citizens of Colonia pay for a public project themselves or whether it was given to them, they end up in the same position with respect to their prosperity. Could this really be the case? Let us examine this more closely. In the first case money stays in the system and prices don't ultimately change, in the latter, money gets added to the economy (and to people's pockets) but prices eventually rise accordingly. The key to reconciling this paradox is to recognize that whenever currency is added to an economy it *devalues all the currency already in the hands of the people.* As Greenspan's money gets spent on the building complex and ends up in the hands of Colonia's people, what money they previously had in their wallets and under their mattresses will no longer have the purchasing power that they once did. The bigger the donation, the bigger the devaluation.

Another way of looking at this is to see that even when Greenspan offered the money as a donation it is completely different from a situation where they brought in raw materials and laborers from abroad, paid the laborers with a different form of currency and then left. No extra money would end up in the hands of the Colonials yet they would have a new building complex. That would be a true "free lunch". Instead, Greenspan is paying the people of Colonia to build it themselves. The Colonials have to earn the money with their labor and materials. Their earnings change the money supply of the country which affects their cost of living. This is why in both situations the Colonials end up with a building complex and the same level of prosperity, no matter if it was funded by Greenspan or themselves.

To reiterate, prices don't increase because the public is becoming more wealthy as a whole; they rise because the *money is being devalued.* When the shipment of dollar shells from Greenspan arrives and gets spent on the building complex every dollar held by every person in Colonia will be worth less than before. The amount of time and energy invested by the Colonials into building the complex is identical no matter how it is funded. That is the real cost of the project, and it will always be shouldered by the people. However what will happen when the economists assess the size of Colonia's economy during the completion of the project? It will have grown. There will be more transactions taking place because materials will be bought and sold. Labor will have been purchased. This would have also been the case if Colonia funded the project themselves, however if Greenspan donated the shells the value of all the transactions in the country will be larger, *when measured in shells* than if Colonia funded the project themselves. The economy of Colonia will have grown in both cases but because we are measuring value in shells, the increase will be greater if the shells were donated. The end result is the same for a Colonial. We can see that the size of economic "growth" does not correlate with prosperity. This is the problem we face when measuring value with a unit whose value is subject to change itself.

What then is really being offered by the government of Greenspan? The Colonial people could have funded the complex independently and ended up at the same level of prosperity. Examining this closely, the dollar shells they handed the Colonials was simply an incentive to marshall their skills and labor to create something of enduring value. In other words, Greenspan's gift simply tapped the potential the Colonials have always had. There is nothing wrong with this arrangement in this particular situation because it resulted in something that was of value to the people. However it points to the fact that an entire population of a country could be "bought" into taking action that may not be in the people's best interest by exploiting the fact that they will either prosper by playing along or suffer by not. It isn't cheap to mobilize a large group of people into action. This is what Greenspan is offering with their donation.

Of course it is rare that an entity, foreign or domestic, would *donate* a large sum of money to another institution or government and expect nothing in return. *Lending* money is instead the common practice because of the value both parties confer on it. It is only fair that the sum be returned with a certain amount of added interest to offset the risk of nonpayment. What would happen if the money was instead lent with interest to the people of Colonia? The money supply (and thus prices) would swell just as before but shrink as the money gets paid back. Once the loan is repaid with interest there will be *fewer* dollars in the Colonial economy than initially. Hence, prices must decrease because people will have fewer dollars and the country will return, once again, to the baseline level of prosperity. The activity that the initial investment of money has stimulated will result in a growth in Colonia's economy. Once the money is paid back the number of dollars in the economy will decrease and measurements of the economy's size will reflect a contraction. Because more of the dollars have left the country as interest, the "size" of the Colonial economy will be smaller. The prosperity of the people, notably, will return to its baseline. As long as the Colonials live in economic isolation this has no bearing on their lives because their prosperity has not been affected in the long run. The point here is to also see that a shrinking economy does not necessarily mean the people are worse off.

It is important to notice that if the Colonials pay Greenspan back, they are effectively working twice as hard than if the funds were given to them with no strings attached. It would be the equivalent of getting paid to build a house for someone and then repaying them the money they spent on it in order to claim it as your own. There is nothing wrong with this arrangement. It is fair to both parties, but how does this compare to a self-funded project. Is borrowing the money worse for Colonia than using its savings?

In order to answer this question we must look at the prosperity of the people over time. We are comparing three different scenarios here: (1) The Colonials fund the project themselves, (2) Greenspan gives Colonia the money and (3) Greenspan loans the money. When all is said and done the Colonials end up with the same level of prosperity. In the first case the Colonials suffer a period of decreased prosperity because they hand over a sizable amount of their savings to the government. They remain in a position of decreased affluence until either prices drop or their income rises as their contributions get spent on the project.

If Greenspan gives Colonia the money there is no period of hardship. In fact they enjoy a period of increased prosperity as income rises. This persists until prices adjust to the increased supply of money.

If Greenspan loans them the money, they enjoy a period of increased prosperity as money enters the system and prices lag. Prices eventually catch up and the original level of prosperity is reestablished. Then, during the repayment period the Colonials suffer the same kind of hardship as in the first case. If the money was donated (scenario #2) the Colonials will not suffer any period of decreased prosperity and will enjoy a period where their income outpaced inflation. That, in fact, was the benefit of Greenspan's generosity. In case 1 and 3 the Colonials had to get by with less for a while. The difference between the two was when the hardship was endured with respect to the completion of the project. Borrowing the money defers the pain of the expenditure until a later time. Paying up front is exactly what it means. The "price" of avoiding the burden for some time is represented by the interest Greenspan is paid.

The takeaway point of this laborious description is that the prosperity of the Colonials will return to its baseline after the project is complete, no matter how it was funded. The size of the economy has no bearing on the prosperity of the citizens. Because it is measured in dollar terms it will be greater if Greenspan gives Colonia the money. This is directly the result of money entering the system and never leaving it. As long as the money never leaves the country measurements of the Colonia's economy will continue to remain at a higher level than before even though the prosperity has returned to baseline.

E). What is Greenspan up to?

As years passed the relationship with Greenspan has offered a great deal of utility to the people and government of Colonia. Although the citizens could fund their public projects themselves, borrowing the money from abroad makes these large expenditures easier to swallow for obvious reasons. When the citizens of the country contribute the money themselves prices take time to adjust to a reduction in money supply. This temporary hardship decreases enthusiasm for large projects. On the other hand, when the money is provided up front, more dollars end up in people's hands *before* prices rise. Colonials and their government become accustomed to *credit*. At some point it becomes clear that although the relationship seems to work, dollars are leaving the country in the form of interest. Wouldn't it be better if these large expenditures could be funded domestically? This would require a large sum of money held by the government itself, a treasury, if you will.

In theory this seems like a great idea but has drawbacks. Although the economy has proven resilient and could shoulder a required contribution from citizens over time to contribute to a treasury this is best done gradually. Prices take time to adjust to a shrinking monetary supply; hitting the people with a large monetary burden to fund a treasury would be very unpopular. Building up that kind of savings would take a lot of time and the need for many of the projects envisioned are exigent. This approach is clearly less palatable when credit is immediately available.

At some point a very shrewd Colonial, JP, proposes a fascinating idea that he claims will solve the problem. JP is a particularly interesting individual because he happens to be the only Colonial to have ever visited Greenspan. While there he was shocked to learn that Greenspan, does not in truth use dollar shells as their currency. Instead, they use a curious, soft, dull yellow metal called *gold* as the basis of their economy. The dollar shells that are being loaned to Colonia are in fact strewn across their shores in the billions. He has kept this secret to himself and has spent much time considering the intricacies of the relationship Colonia has built with Greenspan.

Now, what does your intuition tell you about the situation? Clearly something smells a bit "fishy" about these dollar shells. First there exists an element of manipulation. Colonia has regarded Greenspan as a faithful collaborator in the development of public projects over the years. Colonia trusts Greenspan because Greenspan has seemingly been risking something of significant value each time a loan is offered. Why has Greenspan continued to maintain this deception?

Second, JP has come to understand what money is more deeply than most. The real value of money exists only in the minds of the people who use it. Why should gold be any more valuable than dollar shells? Money only serves as the alphabet of a language of commerce.

Finally, Greenspan was exploiting Colonia through their better understanding of what money really is: a necessity for commerce (they themselves used a different form of money--gold) but still just a shared idea held by many individuals. They risked nothing of value to them but were able to harness the power of a great deal of labor from Colonials. But of what purpose to Greenspan? Greenspan has funded walls, building complexes, infrastructure and dams in Colonia--none of which has been of any benefit to them.

At some point JP put the story together. Greenspan places value on gold, not dollar shells. Gold is dug from the ground. Every major project Greenspan has funded in Colonia required huge excavations to obtain the stone and materials for the dams, roads and buildings. Greenspan wasn't funding construction; it was funding *excavations*. If and when gold was found, Greenspan could easily pay for mining operations with their limitless supply of dollar shells and bring what could be an incredibly valuable amount of commodity into *their* country, while getting Colonials to dig for it.

JP is able to generate some interest in trying an experiment in money by pointing out the very real threat of an economic insurgence from the foreign government that has acted as creditor over the decades. Yes, projects have been funded, but the Colonial money supply has slowly shrunk and so have prices in the country. What is to stop Greenspan from using all the dollars they have accumulated over the years to buy up land and resources at the discounted prices that are now available? The country must act now. Interestingly, JP is fully acting in his country's best interest by warning his people about this threat that he sees not just as potential but inevitable. However he purposefully hides the fact that dollar shells, which are so precious in Colonia, are essentially worthless in Greenspan. As we will soon find out, JP has something else in mind.

F). How to take over an Economy--Step 1: Introduce "Receipt" Money

JP first points out that these "precious" dollars are seashells that are slowly getting eroded through many years of use. He proposes that all the shells be collected from the people and be put in a vault to protect the nation's supply of money. In exchange people will be given receipts for the shells they turn in. The receipts can be exchanged at any time for the shells if they wish, however laws can easily be passed that will mandate that all exchanges of monetary value can and should be done through the exchange of these paper receipts rather than the increasingly fragile dollar shells themselves. It doesn't take long for the people to adopt this new form of currency that can be conveniently folded up in their pockets. Moreover, what would be the point of holding on to shells if only receipts are accepted as payment for stuff?

G). How to take over an Economy--Step 2: Get rid of Commodity-Backed Currency

Once everyone is accustomed to using these receipts JP puts the next, crucial step into action. Up to this point Colonia needed a foreign creditor to provide dollar shells because there weren't any more in the country. However, now that the country is using paper dollars, what would be the harm in creating more paper money whenever a public project needed to be funded? Surely this would be less harmful than relying on a foreign government to provide a literal "boat load" of dollars to pay for a public project. JP asks for permission to use the dollar shell repository to print *extra* dollar bills to fund the next large public works project. He argues that because the country is no longer tied to a limited number of dollar shells, it now has a potentially limitless supply of printed dollars available at any time. Why not exploit this potential that the new monetary system offers?

He admits that although some people may raise their eyebrows at the influx of dollar bills, most will readily accept them as real money. There will be no difference between the ones already in circulation and the new ones that cannot be backed by real dollar shells. Once in the hands of the people, the system will work flawlessly if "unnecessary" attention is not brought to the details. After all, the citizens of Colonia are used to having more dollars enter the system from their foreign benefactor from time to time, so there is no need to announce that dollar bills are now being printed instead.

However it is very clear that the government will be breaking a promise to the people. Recall that anyone with a printed dollar bill has the right to redeem it for a shell at any time. How can this promise be kept if there are more dollar bills than shells? What would happen if everybody decided they wanted their "real money" back and there weren't enough shells to go around? The results would be calamitous. People would lose faith in the currency and the entire system of monetary expansion would have to be abandoned. Additionally, the citizens would lose faith in the government of Colonia itself. There would be riots. Buildings would be stormed. Not every Colonial agrees with every governmental policy but nobody will stand by while their hard-earned money is taken from them.

Top officials convene to decide how to proceed. JP admits that his plan carries the risk of a system-wide collapse but argues that this possibility is very slim. There would be no incentive for anyone to question the validity of the currency because when the dollar bills enter the system the people experience a period of temporary prosperity before prices adjust. Why would anyone complain? Even if a few people want shells for bills there are more than enough shells to cover them in the repository. Once the skeptics get their shells everyone else will be reassured that the money in their hands is indeed legitimate and freely exchangeable for shells as promised.

H). If we are printing money, why do we have to pay it back?

Furthermore, he argues that the money that he prints and adds to the economy should be *repaid, with interest*, just like before. Government officials are surprised at this. Why should the public repay anything? Nothing of value is being loaned, right? There are two main reasons why JP, the mastermind behind this financial coup, insists on repayment. First, JP realizes *that everyone knows that money doesn't grow on trees*. Unless repayment is demanded, people would soon realize that the crisp paper currency they were using was nothing more than ink on paper. Requiring the public to repay the money it was loaned will help to solidify their belief in the currency which is now being artificially expanded.

Second, and more importantly, it is obvious that if money keeps getting printed, the supply of money will continually grow and prices will unavoidably increase. In other words, the value of the dollar would begin to drop. This means the impact of the next "stimulus" would be smaller. Bigger sums of money could be printed of course, but people would eventually start to scratch their heads about why stuff has become so outrageously expensive over the years. What's up with these paper dollars anyway? I want a few of my shells back! That sentiment would be problematic for JP and more difficult to remedy the more printed dollars there are. Government leaders agree.

The government officially sanctions the idea by expanding the role of the dollar shell repository to include the management of funds for public works. The institution becomes a part of the government called *The Colonia Trust*. *The Trust* prints the money for the next public project and the mechanism works flawlessly, just as JP had predicted.

What exactly is going on here? Just as before the economy and prosperity reacted the same way to the introduction of new money into circulation. Prices rise in response to the greater earnings of the people and an equivalent level of prosperity is reestablished. This money does not magically appear in people's mailboxes; it was earned through their labor. Those who were unable or unwilling to participate in this endeavor directly must either work harder to keep up or manage with less. The project gets completed, but who actually paid for it? *The Trust*? No. They simply printed the money. In fact the public did. The public started paying for the project the moment prices started to rise from the newly printed bills that entered circulation. More accurately stated, all the money that was previously in the public's pockets was devalued by *The Trust's* maneuver. The project is being paid for by the drop in the public's prosperity. In order to maintain their prosperity everybody has to work harder. This is a subtle but crucial concept to understand. When you purchase a new car for example, who is paying for it? You are of course. It is true that you are paying for it with money. More accurately you are paying for it with the labor you invested in earning that money. That crucial step is missing in this situation.

If the project gets paid for through the devaluation of the money that existed prior to this monetary expansion, why then does it have to be repaid? Who exactly would suffer if the Colonials didn't pay *The Trust* back? *The Trust* neither sacrificed or risked anything. The money never existed until it was spent!

It may be astounding to realize that if your government is printing money, there isn't a need for repayment. Nobody gets "stiffed" if the money doesn't get "repaid". Repayment helps to maintain the illusion that the money that everyone earns and possesses is safe and secure from the trick being played out right under their noses. However the main utility of repaying printed money is to stabilize the value of the currency so that future monetary expansions will have the same impact. There would be little benefit in printing money that has little or no value. Nevertheless the citizens all chip in to pay back what the *government* has "loaned" them with their now more numerous but less valuable printed dollars. The Colonials are in fact, paying twice: once when everybody must work harder to compete for the influx of new money (or do with less as prices rise) and then during the repayment phase when that same sum of money must leave their hands and return to *The Trust*.

This concept was covered in laborious detail in the previous section, but let us consider one more example to clarify the effect of *The Trust's* maneuver. We can be confused because of the way we use the word "loan". If a friend loaned you $10 you are obligated to repay them that sum because they have labored to acquire that money previously. More importantly, that $10 is part of the money supply of an economy that you both participate in. What if instead he secretly printed that money on a sophisticated printer in a manner that nobody, including you would suspect? You would be able to use those ten dollars in any way you wished and you would feel it fair when he demanded repayment. The difference is that when you spend those ten dollars on a couple of caramel lattes at your local Starbucks, ten dollars *that never existed before* enter circulation. Every single person in the economy is getting cheated because now the money supply in the economy has increased by a tiny fraction and prices will necessarily increase proportionately for everyone. Everybody has suffered slightly for this deception because their wealth has been diminished by a tiny bit. You dutifully pay them the money back through your own labor, but in truth the debt was borne collectively the moment Starbucks accepted the money as payment for your coffee. Your friend has manipulated not just you but the entire population. Your friend has committed one of the most serious crimes in our legal system today and he risks a justifiably harsh punishment because it affects everyone in the country. As we all know this is counterfeiting, and when done with the *intent* to defraud another it carries serious penalties, up to $250,000 fines and decades in federal prison. On the other hand, when sanctioned by a government with a monetary expansion through an institution like *The Trust* it is called a publicly funded project. When a project is "funded" in this manner nothing is actually being loaned. Instead the public is being incentivized to work harder or suffer the pains of not participating.

The money supply is expanding when the bills are printed and then contracting when the public is paying back this loan of artificial currency through its own (very real) labor. Notice that this is exactly the same process as when a foreign government loaned the money to Colonia and then is repaid. However in the minds of every top financial official in Colonia there is a distinct difference between the two situations. When the boat load of dollar shells arrived in Colonia it was thought that Greenspan was risking something of value. The value rested in the *presumed* buying power those shells offered in the foreign country. In *this* case, *The Trust* risks nothing when it infuses the system with printed bills but collects bills that were hard earned from the labor of its people. JP, through his prior knowledge of Greenspan's deception, is the only one who is aware that the two situations are in fact identical. *The Trust* has replaced Greenspan and in doing so the government of Colonia has acquired a new and potent level of control over its people.

We have now arrived at the third use of money. Earlier in this chapter we saw how money is used as a placeholder for value or a representation of what could be purchased with it in an economy. This is how we normally think of the money in our pockets or savings accounts. It is also used to measure the relative value of items or even the size of an economy. Now it is apparent how the government and *The Trust* view it. Once its supply is controlled it becomes a way of manipulating the productivity of its people by incentivizing them to work.

I). With no commodity backed currency The Trust has unlimited power

In truth nothing of value to Greenspan was ever offered to the people of Colonia. JP's system is no different and no less manipulative. When *The Trust* is given the authority to print money without the obligation or ability to back it with shells something potentially very dangerous happens. There are no limits to the amount of money that can be "loaned" to the people. With no inherent risk to *The Trust* combined with its authority to collect repayment of loans of unlimited size, control of the nation's economy has been quietly usurped. Why would a project ever be rejected as exorbitant or impractical, especially if it results in a large windfall for the government in the form of interest? Through its use of *The Trust*, the government is now controlling the economy of Colonia and the livelihood of its citizens. But who is actually calling the shots? The government or *The Trust*? The government solidifies its popularity with voters when the economy is healthy, but it cannot fund projects without *The Trust*. Likewise, The Trust cannot print money without government sanction. Are they working together for the benefit of the people or themselves?

J). Colonials now depend on The Trust for their prosperity

To solidify the *Trust* in the hearts and minds of the people the Government touts the benefits of governmental spending made possible by the *Trust* during periods of monetary expansion. Likewise, during the repayment period when economic activity is subdued and wages fall, the argument for another public project is made and public support is garnered. Soon the public begins to dread the contractionary, or repayment phase and governmental spending becomes nearly continuous in an effort to remain in the expansionary "sweet spot" where wages are growing, unemployment is low and prices are only slightly rising. In order to remain in the sweet spot the government must be perpetually "borrowing" from the *Trust*. Year after year more money gets spent by the government than is collected in taxes and revenue. This "budget deficit" becomes normalized and even welcomed by the country because it necessarily must exist if the conditions of economic "expansion" are to be enjoyed.

At some point there comes another subtle but extremely important shift in the public's perception of the *Trust*. At its inception it was an independent institution designed to protect the precious dollar shells of the country. Then it became a powerful lending institution that eliminated the need for foreign credit. Finally and perhaps most importantly, *The Trust* becomes regarded as a "stabilizing" force in the economy. Whenever the country begins to suffer the pains of an economic contraction during repayment periods *The Trust* is now *expected* to step in and rectify things with a monetary expansion. In other words, what was once clearly seen as the unavoidable result of a period of public spending becomes incorrectly viewed as a dreaded dip in national prosperity that seems to be happening *independently*. *The Trust* is then called upon to mitigate the result of its own actions. The result of the intervention is of course another expansion that will inevitably lead to another contraction.

The cycle continues as *The Trust* accumulates the interest payments on publicly sanctioned debt, but even more diabolically, exchanges its printed money for money that has been earned by the sweat and labor of the people of Colonia. Although *The Trust* is uniquely empowered to print money, it can only do it on the government's terms and only for public expenditures. However, when the money is repaid those dollars collected are no different than the dollars in the pockets of every citizen of the country--*The Trust* can do whatever it wants with them. The money never gets fully paid back though. That would take the economy out of the sweet spot. It's not a matter of concern for JP and his cabal of insiders that are managing *The Trust*. Every dollar they collect is free money for them.

Generation after generation, *The Trust* is called upon to fund project after project in order to "keep the economy growing". We can predict what will happen to the value of the dollar. At the end of every year the government will find that they have borrowed money. The difference between what has been collected as revenue and what it owes to *The Trust* is called the budget deficit. The budget deficit thus represents the amount of credit extended to the government in a given year. Because we are measuring the economy's size in dollars, as long as there is a deficit the economy will tend to "expand". When the government is being fiscally responsible and debt owed to the Trust is being repaid, the economy will likely be "contracting". Predictably, deficit years outnumber surplus years and dollars continue to get printed. The dollar continues to decline in value. Interestingly, Colonials rarely look at it that way. Instead they focus on the prices of things and how they seem to be rising. Inflation becomes normalized. In fact, a small but constant increase in prices, or rate of inflation, is considered now to be a part of a healthy economy. When each year *The Trust* reports that the size of the economy measured in dollars is growing the idea gets further solidified in the minds of the public.

K) Private Banks can now take over

Once inflation becomes a part of life in Colonia another interesting transformation occurs in the minds of its citizens. Until this point there was never a need for a private bank. People kept their money at home and paid for things in cash. Now with the expectation that the price of things will continue to rise, there is an even greater incentive to buy things sooner than later. The government of Colonia authorizes *The Trust* to open a set of banks to allow its citizens to borrow money. Although the government has been borrowing money for decades, private citizens have eschewed this practice. Now however, purchasing things up front has distinct financial advantages. Why wait to accrue savings when you can purchase what you want now for less than what it will cost in the future?

These "private" banks operating under the umbrella of *The Trust* also have access to printed dollars that are not truly backed by dollar shells. Offered to the public as a place to store their money and earn a bit of interest, their real purpose is to loan sums of money to grateful citizens who want access to more capital to fund their dreams and take some chances on out-pacing the constant erosion of their prosperity from "inflation". Just as *The Trust* takes no risk in lending money to the nation, these banks also have very little exposure to risk because the money they lend to citizens has nearly all been printed. In fact, these private banks are just the solution the government has been looking for. Now, rather than having to generate interest in a public project to expand the money supply and keep the economy "humming" the banks can effectively control the money supply by loaning money directly to citizens at an interest rate determined by *The Trust*. Drop the interest rate and more loans get written and more money enters the system. Prices growing too fast? Jack up the rates and more people will choose to repay their loans, debt gets paid back and the monetary supply shrinks and inflation gets curbed.

The Story of Central Banking in our World

The story of Colonia is a simplified but largely accurate story of our world today. *The Trust* represents what exists in nearly every country as a Central Bank. In the United States we have one too; it is called The Federal Reserve, an institution that was brought into existence by an act of Congress in 1913. Exploring the historical details surrounding the creation of a central bank in this country is worthy of volumes and outside the scope of this book. Suffice it to say that there was stiff political opposition to central banking since the inception of our country. Our founding fathers were quite aware of the threat central banking posed to the prosperity of a population. The Federal Reserve Act was passed through intense lobbying on behalf of the banking industry. Their principal argument was that without responsible, regulated and universal lending standards individual banks would continue to fail periodically as they did for decades leading up to that time.

The structure and inner workings of this institution were designed by a consortium of immensely powerful commercial bankers. We can conjecture that the implications of its practices were outside the full grasp of the lawmakers that ratified the act much like they are to many lawmakers and the general population today. Here we will examine the impact of Central Banking on our world using what we have learned from the hypothetical country of Colonia and the relationship it had with *The Trust* so that you can draw your own conclusions about its impact upon us.

The "Fed" is a private institution and acts outside of our Government's control and exacts its will over our economy by regulating the amount of money in it. Although the Chairperson of the Fed is appointed and dismissed by our President, our elected officials have no say in the monetary policy decisions he/she makes. Just like *The Trust*, the Federal Reserve controls the size of our money supply by influencing the lending practices of thousands of commercial and private banks, presumably to prevent imprudent loans from being written. In exchange for abiding by the Fed's rules, these banks get a lifeline to nearly limitless amounts of cash in times of need, i.e. when people all want their deposited money back at the same time. It should be clear that banks will make the most money when they are writing the most loans.

There are differences between our Federal Reserve and *The Trust* in the hypothetical country of Colonia. The Fed is a Non-Profit Organization, required to deposit whatever it collects over its expenses into our Treasury. The real profits are "earned" by the private and commercial banks that operate under the umbrella of The Fed's "restrictions". In the hypothetical country of Colonia, *The Trust* was formed first and private banks later. In our history, the Fed was the brainchild of the most powerful commercial and private bankers in the world at the time. As we will soon see the Fed doesn't make the real money, the bank owners do.

A). Fractional Reserve Lending and the extra Million dollars (finally!)

Today in the United States a bank subscribing to the lending rules imposed by the Federal Reserve is only required to keep approximately 10% of the total amount of money it has lent on hand. So, when you deposit your million dollars into ABC bank, it can then make a loan for $900,000 to someone else. Yet when you check your account balance you still have all your money still there. Where does it come from?

We are finally able to answer the "million dollar question". Just like the Trust in Colonia, ABC bank is allowed to "print" this money on the fly. Of course today there is very little printing going on, these are just numbers typed into a central banking computer the instant that someone signs a promissory note. If that is not unsettling enough, our banking regulations regard the newly written $900,000 loan as an *asset* called a "reserve" because it is effectively an income stream for the bank. *Another* loan can be written based on *this* reserve too. 90% of $900,000 is $810,000. Once someone borrows this amount, it too will be treated as an asset upon which another loan can be written. This occurs iteratively, resulting in a whopping 9 million dollars that can eventually be loaned to other people from the one million you deposited. This is called "fractional reserve lending", and it is considered lawful by today's standards.

Are you able to see what is happening here? Banks make the most money when they are lending the most. The more lending they do, the more money enters the economy. The more money that enters the economy, the more inflation ensues. The more inflation, *the more interested people are in borrowing money.* The more people want to borrow, the more money the banks make. The problem with the system ultimately boils down to the power the banks have to create money out of thin air whenever someone wants to borrow some. We tend to believe that when we are loaned a sum of money from a bank it is no different than getting a loan from a friend or parent. It is not. As described earlier, the money a friend agrees to loan you was earned through their efforts and was part of the monetary supply that you both were using. In contrast, the money that enters your account when you take a loan from a bank did not exist until the moment you signed a promissory note to pay it back. This agreement which results in a stream of income for the bank is now considered an asset that the bank possesses which can be used to write further loans to other borrowers. More importantly to the rest of us, more money is being added to the system. This devalues what money the rest of us possess.

Before moving on it is necessary to acknowledge two points. First is that modern economic theories almost all proclaim that control over a country's money supply is necessary to ensure growth and to avoid recessions. The debate between the "experts" primarily centers upon what level of control serves the participants of an economy best. A fixed supply of money, as Colonia originally had, is generally considered an unviable approach to maintaining liquidity and expansion, especially with a growing labor force because it will invariably lead to deflation. This is uncontested. Even in the hypothetical country of Colonia we could easily extrapolate that a growing population with a fixed number of shells would lead to reduced prices. If prices continued to drop there would be little incentive for people to spend money now rather than later. The productivity of the country would be entirely dictated by how hard its people were willing to work. Production won't stop because people need things to live and enjoy life. Here I am pointing out the very real repercussions of allowing institutions with little or no accountability to the people to regulate our monetary supply with no hard-stops. It also invites us to consider, in a broader sense, whether or not expansion in the way we have experienced it is what we think it is.

Second, the idea that a growing monetary supply necessarily results in higher prices is also justifiably a matter of debate. Many factors are involved in the determination of prices and different theories offer different methods of weighing them. There are numerous historical accounts of inflation and hyperinflation resulting from monetary expansion that support this relationship. I use these examples as sufficient proof of causality. Moreover the arguments used to counter the theory that monetary expansion leads to increased prices often use the example of money simply thrown into the economy. Because there isn't a clear and unavoidable reason to spend it there is no reason to think that prices will increase. However in this chapter we are talking about monetary expansions that come as a result of government funded projects or a private demand for debt. This money comes into the system as a result of it being spent and therefore must enter circulation. Prices must respond to some degree. The conspicuous lack of inflation despite the large infusion of money during the recovery from the 2008 recession is also a matter to consider more closely. The Fed is undeniably in possession of more government debt so we can be assured that the money was in fact created. The stark reality is that wages have not increased. One can argue that the money never made it into the hands of those who would spend it on things that we use to determine price indices, the direct indicator of inflation. Proof of this is in the growing wealth inequality in this country today. This is a matter outside the scope of our discussion here.

How did we get here? When the Federal Reserve was created in 1913 there were limits to how much money could be printed, just as *The Trust* had in our story of Colonia. The Trust promised to redeem their printed bills for actual dollar shells when demanded. Likewise our government agreed to the same arrangement, not with seashells but with gold. When such an arrangement is in place the currency is said to be backed by a commodity or something of *limited availability*. Commodity backing is a necessary step in getting a population to accept a paper currency. No matter how compliant or trusting a person is, you are not going to get them to trade in their gold coins for a piece of paper unless they can reclaim their coins whenever they wish. More importantly a commodity-backed currency provides the hard stop on a government's ability to expand the money supply. This should be the insurance a population has against a complete hijacking of an economy by monetary policy managers and bank owners like what happened in Colonia. A bank cannot create gold out of thin air like paper dollars or numbers in their computers.

In the hypothetical story of Colonia, JP simply expanded the money supply over time and took advantage of the fact that few people knew that there weren't enough dollar shells to go around. This country and many others have followed the same path. Billions of dollars were entering the economy without adequate gold reserves to back them for decades. Nevertheless President Nixon formally put an end to the gold-backed dollar farce in 1971 when through his executive power over the Department of Treasury ended dollar-to-gold convertibility forever. There are no longer any limits to the amount of money that can be printed. With no limits on monetary expansion the inflation->increased demand for loans->monetary expansion->increased inflation "loop" described above can never be dismantled unless we collectively decide not to "buy in" to the system.

It should be clear that this cycle will continue to accrue wealth in the hands of a central bank or the owners of commercial banks. Notice too that the "sweet spot" of economic growth maximizes their take. If the rate of monetary expansion is too low, there will be little inflation and less incentive for people to buy now rather than later. This will decrease the demand for loans—bad for the bank profits. On the other hand, if monetary expansion is too great hyperinflation will result. This diminishes the value of all dollars, including the ones held by the bank owners.

The Fed has, for a very long time, publicly expressed their aim to achieve an economic growth rate of approximately 2%--the sweet spot. A target of 2% growth is a number echoed by other central banks around the world. This is easily accepted by the public. After all, why would we resist growth? Most respected economists tell us that a 2% rate of growth seems prudent to avoid a jump in inflation and a period of stagnation for the reasons above. However are we too readily playing along with this idea? Perhaps the "sweet spot" is not as sweet as we think it is. Could it instead be just the right amount of carrot and stick required to keep us locked in the system and not the universally beneficial target we should be striving for?

Let's take a closer look at what we have learned from our examination of Colonia's monetary system and how its growth affects prosperity. When we hear that the economy or Gross Domestic Product (GDP) is growing at the target rate it gives us confidence that we are on the right track and those in charge are doing the right things. We also assume that a growing economy measured by these terms should be good for most people. However, we are measuring GDP in dollars, a unit that continues to shrink in value as we finance our public and private debt by creating money. The average annual inflation rate has been more or less matching the rate of GDP growth. In other words, some of the growth we are measuring is undoubtedly from the accumulation of more debt by our population and not an increase of our collective prosperity.

The population and labor force are also growing over time, on average about 1-2% per year. It should be evident that we are basically dividing up the same sized pie into more and smaller pieces. The size of an average piece of the pie is analogous to our prosperity; the only real thing we are concerned about. In other words, when we measure the size of our entire economy in dollars it is in fact growing, yet when we measure how we as *individuals* are fairing the opposite trend is in play. This is admittedly a simplified model of what is going on as skeptics to this idea will be quick to point out, but how does it compare with your own personal experience and what you observe around you?

The 2% target growth rate is not at all what we generally think it is. We picture ourselves climbing a mountain of prosperity at a certain pace which we call our economy's rate of growth. As long as we have had growth we can be assured that we are further up the mountain. A more accurate model is that we are all on treadmills, the rate of growth being the pace selected by our central banks. They are not turning a dial to set the pace. Instead they are incentivizing us to run at a certain speed; because we are on a treadmill we are not actually going anywhere, we are just making the tread move faster. As money enters the system through the issue of debt we run a bit harder to compete for the new money. To "get ahead" we must work harder to stay ahead of the treadmill's speed. If we lapse in our effort we will end up behind or fall off completely. The point is most of us are running just to stay in place. The treadmill is working against all of us. Some, but not all of the effort that we expend to remain in place is being harnessed by the banking system itself. If the fruits of all of our labor went directly into someone else's hands we would quickly realize that we were being used. Instead we are able to acquire things that we need or desire from our efforts. Because we are all more or less part of the same system we may point out the injustices from uneven opportunities and the inequalities between us but we rarely are able to appreciate how the system extracts from us all. We have become accustomed to running against the pace of the treadmill track that we are moving ourselves.

How can we appreciate the amount of effort the system is extracting from us? One insightful way is to first acknowledge that it takes time and labor to earn money. In general, if you work harder for longer you will earn more. When a bank collects on a million dollar mortgage over 30 years at a rate of 4% it gets paid about $720,000 in interest over the term of the loan. How much effort did they exert to earn this sum? We may argue about how to arrive at an accurate estimate, but we can all agree that it is less than the effort the borrower made to earn that money. This inequity represents the added effort we expend to run in place.

B). The "money" in our system isn't money, it's Debt

This is perhaps the most confusing aspect of how our system of money actually functions today. Over a century ago, prior to the advent of the Federal reserve, "money" was held in the hands of citizens and institutions alike. At that time there was roughly 50 billion dollars in the American economy. We can roughly equate that time in our history with the conditions in Colonia just prior to the advent of *The Trust*. Back then money was wealth. Today there is about 400 times that amount. Today the money in the system is more accurately a representation of *how much debt has been created*, because most of the money in our economy has been brought into existence through the extension of loans from our banks. When you get a loan you are not being handed a sum of money that was previously held in someone else's possession; it is being created for you by the bank. As you labor to repay this debt your loan balance slowly approaches zero until the day you make your last payment. The bank, you may think, rejoices when this happens. This is not the case because, as described above, they have long since made a huge profit on this money you have earned for them. Not only have they collected the one million dollars you borrowed plus interest, they have also collected on the other eight million they were authorized to "lend" once you agreed to pay them back.

Imagine for a moment that everyone in the country decided that they would stop taking loans and diligently work to pay back all their debt to our loaning institutions. This would take some time, likely decades. All mortgages, car loans, educational loans, credit card debt, etc. would be zero. The loans the banks have written were "assets" that are no longer in existence. How would we measure the size of the economy at this point? If we counted up the number of "things" in the country it would be sizable and representative of a hard-working nation. However, what happens when we attempt to measure our GDP in dollar terms as the sum of expenditures? The number would be far less. We would return to a position analogous to Colonia before *The Trust* took over. Does that mean the wealth of the country has taken a huge hit? Of course not. We would still have all the things that we have worked for, there would just be a lot less money in the system. This is another way to see the futility of measuring an economy in dollars, especially if most of the dollars have been "printed" to satisfy a need for credit.

The relationship we have with the banking industry is not unlike what the hypothetical nation of Colonia had with Greenspan. The people of Colonia labored to repay the "dollars" that the country of Greenspan considered mere trinkets. For the Colonial people, the situation changed little when *The Trust* was given the authority to print dollar bills. How do you suppose a bank regards the money it loans to us when it can bring it into existence instantly through the stroke of a pen (or keys on a keyboard) whenever we agree to borrow from them? Certainly much differently than we regard our own money in our wallets, in our accounts or in the equity in our homes--if we are fortunate enough to "own" one.

Banks risk very little when they loan us "money" to put into our accounts. However, by agreeing to pay them back we are dedicating our time and labor to fulfilling our obligation to the contract. We are paying them with our lives. Moreover we as borrowers know that if we falter in our repayment our homes and cars and collateral will be repossessed by the bank. These are items of real value to us, not just numbers in a computer. Furthermore we are motivated to avoid the dreaded dip in our credit score, our ticket into the cyclical credit system that we have become dependent upon. How can we keep up with everyone else if we have no access to credit like they do?

We put a lot on the line when we sign a promissory note with a bank. Does this seem like an equitable arrangement? At the surface it does. They loan us X dollars. We pay them back $X plus some interest. However it is important to notice how we regard the risk the bank takes as the lender. We tend to view the bank's role in this arrangement as how we would view ourselves if we were in their place. We would think long and hard about handing over $X to another party because we have earned that money from our time and effort and not by printing money. Moreover if the transaction goes poorly we do not have a lifeline to more resources like the banks do. How would the people of Colonia have regarded Greenspan if they knew the dollar shells they were loaned weren't worth anything to them? More importantly, how much trust would they have put in Greenspan once they realized what they were doing?

Defenders of the banking industry often cite the enormous benefit they offer by allowing us to pay for very important things like a home or an education. These are things that the average person could not afford to purchase with their savings alone. However, are we looking at this correctly? Why are these things so expensive to begin with? The price of higher education has grown astronomically since the time our government began to back student loans. This arrangement provides a guarantee to banks that the loans taken by high school kids to go to college would be paid back by the taxpayer if necessary. Colleges would not be able to charge what they do if students did not have access to credit. Similarly, the price of homes is extremely sensitive to the mortgage rates banks are offering. Home prices go up when mortgage rates go down. In other words, the availability of credit is undoubtedly driving the price of these items. Is the banking industry the "solution" to the unaffordability of these essential items or are they providing the only solution to a problem *they are creating themselves*?

C) Is there a Real Solution?

Before discussing solutions it is necessary to decide whether or not there really is a problem. There is an overwhelming amount of evidence that suggests the monetary system and our dependence on credit benefits our lending institutions at our expense. They are controlling both the spigot and the drain and thus dictate how much water is in the tank--water level being the size of the economy which we are being told is a reflection of our prosperity.

We are in the identical position the citizens of Colonia were in after *The Trust* expanded their power. In contrast, the citizens of *Greenspan* were in a much different situation. Their economy was based on gold, a substance with limited availability. Currency in Greenspan, whether it was in the form of actual gold coins or gold-backed paper, would have prevented their banks from creating money whenever there was a need for debt. Why can't we recreate the same situation in our world today? In theory we could. In other words, bringing back the gold standard would make it impossible for banks to devalue our currency every time they issue a loan. They would be forced to part with something of limited availability and of actual value to them.

Though this idea has been floated by numerous economists and politicians over the decades it is generally met with indifference or stiff opposition for a number of reasons, including citing the unavoidable economic "contraction" that will result when easy credit goes away. Because there is a limited amount of gold there would only be a limited amount of credit that could ever be offered. Moreover with a limited amount of gold, prices of things will inevitably start to decline as more things get produced. This would be deflation, anathema in a society that regards capitalism as the unassailable method of ensuring productivity. Though this point is valid, it is important to remember that arguments against a gold standard are arguments for a currency that has no intrinsic value and is completely under the control of a private institution. Nevertheless, there has been little political will to reign in the power of our central bank for potential reasons that we will explore later in this chapter.

Gold is a unique substance and plays an interesting role on this planet. It has intrinsic value because of its properties as a metal that endow it with utility in industry, electronics and even dentistry. More importantly, it is also recognized as valuable and something desirable by large populations globally. Furthermore it is rare (and thus valuable) enough to be quite useful in transactions. As of today in 2020 we can easily carry $100,000 of gold in a small satchel. The same is not true of silver or copper. Though platinum is rare enough to serve as a means of exchange in larger transactions it does not have the global appeal that gold does. History has demonstrated that gold is an ideal commodity to back currency in even the largest of economies.

Reinstituting the gold standard in our world seems like a lofty goal despite the obvious utility and protection it would offer the vast majority of people. It is interesting to note that despite the fact that gold has been relegated to one of several precious metals used in jewelry or occasionally held as one of several hedges against inflation or economic instability it continues to maintain a surprising amount of value. When the convertibility of dollars to gold ended in August of 1971 the price of an ounce of gold was $37.50. Up to that point the price of gold was fixed at that price because it acted as the basis of the value of a dollar. In other words, until 1971 it was subject to devaluation from monetary expansions just like the dollar was. Since that time the price of gold has been determined by basic market forces. Today, as of June, 2020 an ounce of gold is around $1700. Of course the price has significantly risen because of inflation, just like everything else when we measure value in dollars. However, how does it compare to other things, like widely touted "investment vehicles"?

In the 49 years since 1971 the value of gold has increased by a factor of 45.3. This is equivalent to an average appreciation of 8.1% per year. During this same period, the S&P 500 has gone from a value of 99.03 to 3097.7. This is an increase of approximately 31.3 times or 7.3% per year on average. In contrast to an investment in gold the S&P also pays out dividends to their stockholders. Although the average dividend payout for S&P companies has been higher in the past it has been approximately 2% since 1991. This makes the S&P a better investment than gold by about 1.3% if the totality of dividends were reinvested into the market.

The performance of the S&P is widely considered an estimable goal for professional investors. This kind of performance has never been sustainably matched by even the best of pundits and fund managers. Why has the value of gold, an inert metal, increased nearly as much as the value of the greatest for-profit corporations that utilize the creativity and ingenuity of the best minds to create products and services for an ever-evolving public palate? There are likely a number of complex reasons, all outside the scope of this book. However this remarkable fact should give us reason to pause. There are many media channels devoted to broadcasting analysis of market dynamics and investor sentiment. How often is gold mentioned as an investment vehicle in this context? Usually it is brought up as a way to diversify and as a hedge against market uncertainty. More often than not when gold is compared to the stock market we are told unequivocally that investing in the market has been far more lucrative. This is true but the difference may not be as big as we commonly believe. This is because comparisons are most often made over a hundred year period or longer. This is an erroneous approach to making a meaningful comparison. Gold's "value" in dollars was tied to the dollar itself until 1971. As has been discussed at length previously, the "value" of gold was being effectively devalued just like the dollar was. Any serious investigation would only involve the period since that time.

If people decided to purchase more gold its price will undoubtedly rise even more, further making it a more enticing vehicle for investment and savings. This will naturally decrease demand for other products and services. Increasing demand for gold would likely have a deflationary effect on the economy up to a point. Of course there is a possibility that unmitigated demand for gold could result in a "bubble" (like in 1980) however it is far less likely that the average person would borrow money to buy gold in large quantities. Though getting in early on a speculative gold bubble would be enticing, most people have very little savings and disposable income to begin with. It would not be practical for the average person to appropriate a lot of their resources towards purchasing a dull, soft metal that cannot get you to work or provide a roof over your head. Moreover no bank will loan a person money to buy and hold gold. However the option of buying even a small amount of gold with its track record of outpacing the stock market would make people think twice before shelling out for a new car or a family vacation. Demand for such things would drop and so would their cost. As explained above, with less inflation there is less incentive to borrow. We can therefore postulate that our lending institutions would prefer that we continue to use our money to purchase items with limited lifecycles and not save our money in the form of gold. Are we being biased against taking such action by the lack of coverage surrounding this remarkable phenomenon? Probably. A harder question to answer is whether or not this is being done intentionally.

Why has the value of gold nearly kept pace with the venerable S&P 500 and other stock indices despite the conspicuous indifference the financial pundits have towards it? Like all items in a market driven economy, it has to do with supply and demand. There has always been a healthy demand for gold privately, especially in other countries like India and China. Not surprisingly, private citizens own most (about 75%) of the gold on the planet largely in the form of jewelry. The rest is held by Central Banks and government treasuries. They have notably been expanding their reserves since 2010. The International Monetary Fund (IMF), a global institution that ostensibly acts as an international bank to nearly 200 different countries and their central banks, is the third largest owner of gold in the world (the U.S. treasury being the largest). Its approximately 2,800 metric tons of gold carried a value of 137 billion dollars in 2019. Compare that with its total reserves of 290 billion dollars. Roughly one third of the IMF's reserves are in the form of gold. How does that compare to your portfolio, if you are lucky enough to have one?

The resilience of gold's value over the years is worthy of contemplation. Just like the value of equities, gold's value is determined by supply and demand and has been subject to peaks and troughs over the decades too. Obviously there are periods where an investment of gold would have been unwise in retrospect. The same holds true for the stock market. The *supply* of gold has been rising, especially since 2005. We can thus conclude that the demand for gold has outpaced production. Industrial demand for gold accounts for approximately 15% of the total demand. In contrast, private demand for gold in the form of jewellery and bullion accounts for 75% of the total. Private and industrial demand for gold has been relatively constant. On the other hand, central bank and investor demand for the metal has been increasing for the last decade, coinciding with the monetary expansion orchestrated in response to the great recession of 2007-08. Investment demand for gold has more than doubled in the last three decades.

What sort of investment mentality would result in such a long cycle? One possibility is that there is a widely but quietly held sentiment that in the long run, gold will always be a very safe bet. If anything, the data proves that our central banks subscribe to this idea more than anybody else. Moreover, the greater the number of people who feel this way, the greater the advantage there will be to buying it. Imagine what would have happened if we had taken the cue from central banks and invested more in gold over the last decade or so. Clearly, gold's appreciation would have been even more impressive than it is now. Unless a new substance strikes the world's fancy there is no reason to believe that gold, *over the long run,* will not continue to appreciate at a higher rate than most things, just as history has proven. It would be difficult for the market to compete with a substance that everybody wants that is only available in limited supply. Obviously if you made a big purchase of Amazon or Apple stock at their inception you would have fared far better than if you bought gold. Few of us are that lucky or that prescient. Here we are talking about comparisons between gold and the market as a whole. Is it possible that gold is slowly being amassed by shrewd investors and central banks in our world because they know that the monetary system they have built must inevitably collapse from their regular expansion of our monetary supply?

As stated above, a growing general interest in gold is problematic for a central bank that wants to consolidate its power. What would happen to the public's interest in currency if people started to hold more of their wealth in gold? We can only speculate, but it would definitely make the return of a gold standard much easier to facilitate and easier to envision collectively if most people already had some gold in their pockets. How would that sit with central bankers who have the unique ability to create trillions of dollars at will but cannot bring an ounce of gold into existence with the power we have granted them?

D) Are we being told the truth about our Banking System?

The story of Colonia, Greenspan and *The Trust* can help to explain the history of our own system of money. Greenspan was using the people of Colonia to dig for gold. *The Trust* similarly utilized the labor of the Colonials to amass great wealth. Now that we have a general idea of how it works, what is the *intention* of the modern day banking system that has been built for us by the bank owners themselves? The answer to this question depends upon what your biases are. The narrative that we are subjected to overwhelmingly paints the Federal Reserve and other Central Banks as a safety net that can intervene with credit when times get tough and adjust our money supply to keep the economy moving forward at a healthy pace. Is this in fact a fair and accurate depiction?

Let us begin by examining the undisputed facts.

- The value of a dollar today is twenty five times less than it was in 1913 when the Fed was created. This is due directly from the year over year expansion of the money supply and the ensuing devaluation of our currency. This money was not dug from the ground like gold or collected from the sands like dollar shells. It was brought into existence by the issue of loans to individuals or as bonds to fund government spending. As we learned early on in this chapter, the growth of an economy does not require growth of its money supply. Whether you believe that this infusion of money was necessary for our country to grow or not, the fact still remains that today's dollar would have been worth 4 cents in 1913. Does this magnitude of currency devaluation seem necessary or is it the result of an unquestioned policy of monetary expansion that serves another purpose?

- Commercial banks operating under the umbrella of the Fed partake in the system of Fractional Reserve Lending described above. To reiterate, a bank is able to loan nine dollars for every dollar it receives as a deposit. The nine dollars do not exist anywhere *until someone decides they want to borrow them.* Does this seem like a responsible mechanism to regulate our money supply? Is it reasonable to think that this arrangement between bank and borrower will not have repercussions across the whole economy? Yes, it allows for easy credit but who or what else makes out in this scheme?

• The Federal Reserve and its massive network of lending institutions offer a great deal of safety to each individual bank in the network. Banks may borrow from each other to ensure they stay afloat, even when they are massively leveraged. Compared to pre-Fed days we rarely hear of an individual bank failing. However, this doesn't mean the system is unsinkable. In fact, the system is designed, whether intentionally or not, to remain in its default state of aggressive loaning until *everything* topples, as it did as recently as in 2008. When depositors and investors realized too much bad debt had been written during the housing bubble, large institutions finally collapsed. The economy faltered but recovered over the next decade through stimulus packages that were, of course, funded by the taxpayer. It is true that "governmental intervention" (bailouts) were necessary to avoid a crisis at the time, but is it possible that this was an eventual certainty kept hidden from the public? When an individual bank fails the losses are suffered by those who have deposited their money in that bank. When there exists the threat of a large number of banks failing simultaneously (like in 2008) the only recourse is a direct injection of liquidity from the Fed which is funded by everybody. The banks regain their footing and we, our children and grandchildren all pay for it. Is it unreasonable to think that these types of "crises" had been foreseen as an unavoidable eventuality by those who designed the system in the first place?

Are the Fed and the other Central Banks of the world working to protect us from the pains of inevitable economic devastations that occur on their own? Or do they in fact engineer these kinds of downturns through their independent control of our money supply so that they must eventually intervene to rectify things through the power with which we have endowed them and in so doing further validate their necessity? There are no "sources" we can reference to answer the questions posed here. We must rely on our intuition.

Though the three points listed above are irrefutable, we cannot conclude that the Central Banking system has always been self-serving. However, we also cannot be certain that it hasn't. For the purposes of discussion, let us assume for the moment that the vastly wealthy and powerful bank owners that conceived and implemented this system knew that the power to control our money supply would gradually siphon off the earnings of an entire country as it became addicted to limitless credit over generations. Let us also assume that they predicted that the system would work flawlessly until it didn't, and when it failed they would have the unique power to salvage the economy with further monetary expansions backed by the taxpayer. Where would that lead in our examination of our history and present state?

E) How does a Central Banker view world events?

If we were to examine the situation from a central banker's perspective we would regard global events in the context of debt because the banking system reaps the greatest benefit when its country's needs exceed its resources. What kind of event creates the greatest and most urgent need for resources? Aside from a huge natural disaster we can all agree it would be a *war*. War requires a nation to redirect their young adults away from the creation of goods and services and into military service. There is the cost of munitions, fuel, care for the wounded and ultimately, reparations. The bigger and the longer the war the better... if you were a central banker.

A country at war must mobilize a great deal of assets and labor urgently. This naturally requires a great deal of money. If it isn't already abundantly clear, the country doesn't borrow this money from its central bank, it actually borrows it from its future earnings and labor of its citizens--the central bank just facilitates this through a monetary expansion.

F) Were Central Banks involved in WWI?

Is it possible that elite members of our banking system wield power over geopolitical dynamics and foreign policy? This may be obvious to some but to many this approaches absurdity. A government for and by the people seems too powerful and independent to be influenced by financiers and monetary policy makers. If banking insiders had any influence over our elected officials the media would bring immediate public attention to it. In order for this kind of treachery to take place it would require the hidden collaboration of a very small group of extremely influential persons in government, central banking and the media. This would be a conspiracy, which many believe would be impossible today. There is, however, a high probability that it has happened more than once in the past.

One of the most researched and documented incidences of the potent influence of banking interests upon our foreign policy through the use of the media concerns the circumstances around America's entry into the first World War. WWI, The War to end all Wars or "The Great War" was waged between 1914 and 1919. The assassination of Archduke Franz Ferdinand, heir to the Austro-Hungarian empire by a Serbian nationalist is widely known as the spark that threw the world into its first "global" conflict. A full analysis of the political and social climate in Europe at the time is a topic worthy of volumes and obviously far outside the scope of this book. Nevertheless this event brought Russia, England, France and Belgium to war against the Austro-Hungarian Empire and Germany a week later. The United States remained neutral for three full years before being swept into action to defend its allies, largely due to the public sentiment around the sinking of *The Lusitania*.

The Lusitania, a massive British liner with 195 American civilians on board, was sunk by a German U-boat attack in May of 1915. Most history books depict this as an unprovoked attack on a civilian ship, justifying American military intervention which eventually came two full years later, however the details around this event are far more mysterious than is commonly known. Here I would like to outline the circumstances and integral players around this event using mainly references from the Congressional Record and the memoirs of then Secretary of State, William

Jennings Bryan. A full account of this part of our history has been masterfully researched and written by various authors over the decades.

The Lusitania, prior to setting sail from NY, was loaded with tons of weaponry including six million rounds of ammunition purchased with funds raised for England and France through JP Morgan's investment house. This was done in broad daylight with the ship's manifest a matter of public record. German dock workers notified the German embassy in New York that this was happening in full view. It resulted in an immediate response by the German government that rightfully protested that using such a ship to transport weapons was in direct violation of international neutrality treaties. The American government denied this was taking place. The German government then appealed to the American people directly, attempting to place ads in newspapers urging them not to book passage on *The Lusitania* as it represented a strategic target that would fall under German attack. *The U.S. State Department prevented these warnings from running.* When these ads failed to appear in print the editor of a German owned newspaper, George Viereck, the person who attempted to place the ads on behalf of the German government, eventually obtained an interview with then Sec. State William Jennings Bryan shortly before *The Lusitania* set sail and appealed to him to intervene directly. Author Colin Simpson of The Lusitania (Little Brown & Co, 1972) writes that Bryan, when confronted with the ship's manifest, agreed to permit the ad to run and furthermore promised to urge President Wilson to publicly warn Americans not to travel. No such warning came from our President and only one newspaper, the *Des Moines Register,* managed to run the German government's warning[4] in time.

At this time J. P. Morgan, one of the chief architects of the newly created Federal Reserve, was profiting from selling English and French bonds to American investors to raise money for their war effort against Germany. In addition, the two countries spent significant sums on products purchased from companies in Morgan's control. When it became clear that Germany was nearing victory through their control of shipping lanes in the Atlantic with their U-boats, Morgan's income stream was threatened. Moreover, if the Allies lost the war Morgan and his investors stood to lose a tremendous amount because the bonds they had raised on their behalf would have been worthless. England, France and the American investing house decided that their causes could only be saved if the United States entered the war against Germany. At the time this seemed a practical impossibility as Woodrow Wilson, approaching reelection, was riding a broad anti-war sentiment sweeping the country. This all changed when *The Lusitania* sank, killing all 195 Americans on board. In response, President Wilson immediately sent a letter of outrage to the Imperial German government that was widely quoted in the press. Secretary of State Bryan, who was intimately aware of the circumstances and our government's complicity behind this event, wrote this note directly to the President (quoted from Bryan's memoirs) two days later on May 9, 1915:

> "Germany has a right to prevent contraband going to the Allies, and a ship carrying contraband should not rely upon passengers to protect her from attack--it would be like putting women and children in front of an army."

As history eventually proved, his curt rebuke of the administration did little to veer our country away from military engagement two years later.

Morgan had in the meantime purchased control over major segments of the media and flooded the public with pro-war editorial for the next two years with powerful effect. Morgan's influence over the media did not go unnoticed at the time. Two months before the United States eventually entered the war, Texas Representative Francis Oscar Callaway included this statement in the Congressional Record on February 9, 1917:

> "In March, 1915, the J.P. Morgan interests, the steel, shipbuilding and powder interests and their subsidiary organizations, got together 12 men high up in the newspaper world and employed them to select the most influential newspapers in the United States and sufficient number of them to control generally the policy of the daily press of the United States.
>
> These 12 men worked the problem out by selecting 179 newspapers, and the began, by an elimination process, to retain only those necessary for the purpose of controlling the general

policy of the daily press throughout the country. They found that it was only necessary to purchase the control of 25 of the greatest papers. The 25 papers were agreed upon; emissaries were sent to purchase the policy, national and international, of these papers; an agreement was reached; the policy of the policy of the papers was bought, to be paid for by the month; an editor was furnished for each paper to properly supervise and edit information regarding the questions of preparedness, militarism, financial policies and other things of national and international nature considered vital to the interests of the purchasers.

This contract is in existence at the present time, and it accounts for the news columns of the daily press of the country being filled with all sorts of preparedness arguments and misrepresentations as to the present condition of the United States Army and Navy, and the possibility and probability of the United States being attacked by foreign foes.

This policy also included the suppression of everything in opposition to the wishes of the interests served. The effectiveness of this scheme has been conclusively demonstrated by the character of stuff carried in the daily press throughout the country since March, 1915. They have resorted to anything necessary to commercialize public sentiment and sandbag the National Congress into making extravagant and wasteful appropriations for the Army and Navy under the false pretense that it was necessary. Their stock argument is that it is 'patriotism.' They are playing on every prejudice and passion of the American people."

Nevertheless, America entered WWI on April 6, 1917. War expenditures were fueled by monetary expansion engineered by the newly created Federal Reserve. Between 1915 and 1920 the monetary supply doubled and the value of our currency dropped by nearly 50%.

G) Would we wage war if we couldn't afford to?

From a practical standpoint, large, drawn out conflicts are only possible if there is a Central Bank in play. No population likes wartime, but it will endure it out of fear and patriotism. However if the citizens of a country are asked to fund military action with their hard earned savings, we can be assured that there will be far less public support for such activity. The U.S. has spent over six trillion dollars on the wars in Iraq and Afghanistan following 9/11. That is roughly 300 billion dollars per year. How much public support would have been marshalled if every man, woman and child in this country were required to contribute one thousand dollars a year of their own money to fund these wars for 19 years (and counting)?

Through their unmitigated authority to print currency, a central bank allows people to fight now and pay later. Is it unreasonable that central banks, functioning without accountability to any authority, government or otherwise, would welcome every opportunity to exert this power, especially when it is so lucrative to them? Is it possible that they hold sway over more than just our money supply? Conventional history books paint our species' long tradition of conflict as good vs. evil or liberty vs. tyranny while characterizing dictators and their ideologies as threats to the greater good. Could the real threat be insidious and more diabolical? After all, as explained earlier, central banks are not confined by borders or allegiance to governments that inevitably rise and fall.

H) The Role of the Media

When we openly question this possibility it will eventually lead to a very difficult position for all of us that live in a free society. If the Central Banks conspire to keep the world in a perpetual state of conflict to further their own interests it would necessarily require the cooperation of the media. This is usually where diligent inquiry comes to a screeching halt in our minds. We are all aware of numerous countries, which we generally consider to be unfriendly, that inundate their population with propaganda and misinformation to subdue their citizens into accepting their authority. Indeed, the outspoken journalists in those places suffer the most brutal punishments of all. Questioning the integrity of our media is scary because we are testing the very foundation of our idea of liberty. A free press is codified in our own Constitution in the very first Amendment after all. It can be easy to regard this kind of investigation into our own democracy as unpatriotic or as an effort to discredit our nation as a whole.

On the other hand, the preamble to our Constitution explicitly expresses that the intention of our forefathers was, among other things, to form a *more perfect* union. Achieving perfection was astutely placed outside of human capability, however they acknowledged that maintaining a nation of justice and freedom is a dynamic process that requires constant adjustment, refinement and reflection. A 240-year-old structure needs to have its foundation checked from time to time.

Two very different models of how the world operates are under consideration here. One is the conventional view where skirmishes and world wars erupt as a result of the clash of ideologies or out of necessity to contain overt aggression. In this view, central banking has allowed us to pay for these wars by borrowing from our children and grandchildren while keeping us safe and secure today.

The other is one where a hidden few are pulling the strings through their control of our lifeblood: money. If commercial bank owners were involved in warmongering they stand to make a tremendous amount of wealth through central banking, a device of their own making and explicitly supported by our governments. Banking profits are maximized during times of war. Are they in fact behind much of the conflict on this planet? The model you choose to subscribe to entirely rests upon your perception of the media. We can all agree that some "media" sources distort the facts, but is it possible that all mainstream sources are complicit in *suppressing* such foundational truths about our world? Before answering this question it is imperative to become aware of any bias you may have against questioning the integrity of the most valuable institution in a free country: a free press. This is would be *Source of Bias #6: Presumptive legitimacy granted to a source because of personal feelings.* Note, there is no right answer here. The intent is to form an opinion free of bias and nothing more.

The information presented in this chapter is complex and open to interpretation. There are ample opportunities for bias to arise in our minds before we even consider whether formulating an alternative paradigm to that which most of us have adopted is worthwhile. Unwillingness to look closer (*Source of Bias #2*), unbalanced inquiry (*Source of Bias #3*), overconfidence in an adopted opinion (*Source of Bias #5*) would have all been in play in our lives with regard to this system that we have been born into. Ultimately, however, we have had to rely upon a free press to report on all vital matters accurately and free of these biases for us. Are we granting too much legitimacy to the press when we dismiss the possibility of a long-standing conspiracy involving central banks and our government?

This is where we are left. We cannot rely on the intrepid investigative journalist breaking the story if we are questioning the integrity of the media itself. We must rely on our own intuition. What is it telling you?

CHAPTER 7:

Please don't bring it up again

*"You shall no longer take things at second or third hand, nor look
through the eyes of the dead, nor feed on the spectres in books,
You shall not look through my eyes either, nor take things from me,
You shall listen to all sides and filter them from yourself"*
                                                    —Walt Whitman

I f there is a topic that polarizes people more than any other it is 9/11. I
fully expect that as you read those two numbers your mind immediately
jumped to one or more of a number of common reactions ...

- Can we please let it go already?
- I won't stand by and listen to anyone who disrespects our fallen heroes!
- I've already heard all the "Conspiracy Theorist" arguments and my
  mind is made up.
- I was waiting for you to bring this up, THANK YOU!
- My [*relative/friend/associate*] is an [*engineer/architect/contractor/very
  smart person*] and (he/she) assures me that there is nothing wrong
  with what we have been told.
- Anyone who believes our own government is behind something like
  this is batshit crazy!
- Anyone who believes a couple dozen "terrorists" with boxcutters is
  behind something like this is batshit crazy!
- I lost loved ones on that day. Please go away!
- I lost loved ones on that day. Please help me to spread the truth!

- There are no witnesses to a conspiracy. It's just pure speculation.
- There are hundreds of witnesses to a conspiracy. Why won't anybody listen to them?
- Of course it wasn't an inside job. I was there. I saw the planes hit. I know what happened.
- Of course it was an inside job. Yes, I saw the planes hit but anybody can see that all three buildings are being blown to smithereens.
- If there were a conspiracy the media would have brought this to our attention a long time ago.
- I've read every page of the official 9/11 Commission report and the supporting documents from the National Institute of Standards and Technology (NIST) and they are absolutely valid. End of story.

The sentiments listed above were not meant to be comprehensive. (The biggest reaction omitted is the "I don't know and I don't care" position which has no place in a book about honing one's intuition and objectivity. Note that if you adopt *that* position you are accepting the conventional narrative by default--that is what convention is after all.) It is likely that there is at least one statement above that represents your position at this moment and another that represents the diametric opposite. This is natural of course, because what really happened on 9/11 is debatable. Regardless of how certain you are in your position, there are others who feel just as strongly that you are wrong. This is what I mean by debatable.

No matter where you happen to stand on 9/11 it is always worthwhile to reconsider your position from time to time if you have any interest in forming "a more perfect" understanding of this transformative event. For those of us who subscribe to the conventional narrative, the idea of a conspiracy behind 9/11 is a nuisance, an absurd reality held by the unhinged that somehow refuses to die. Others, who are convinced that three buildings in Manhattan were in fact blown up in front of our very eyes, regard the first group with the same level of frustration. It stands to reason that only one of these groups is right.

As stated in the introduction to this book, the intent here is not to educate but to stimulate. I do not intend to profess *what* we should believe; I only wish to investigate *why* we believe what we believe. It is for that reason that 9/11 is very relevant here. The fact that there is such deep polarity about this topic begs us to investigate its origin. Is this divide due to differences in our understanding of metallurgy, structural engineering or dynamic vs. static loads? Or is it more a difference in the trust we place in the sources who expounded the theory that we subscribe to? We may disagree about the applicability of basic principles of engineering but the vitriol and antimony between opposite sides of this issue arise from the threat the other side poses to our faith in the source of our information. The topic of 9/11 is charged largely due to *Source of Bias #6: Presumptive legitimacy granted to a source because of personal feelings.*

Disagreement about 9/11 is much like the conflict between Jack and Lenny in Chapter 1. Jack saw Lenny's refutation of Ed's conclusions as a challenge to *Ed's integrity* and not simply a different (and impersonal) interpretation of what was observed. If you believe in the conventional narrative regarding 9/11 you may be willing to entertain an alternative explanation for a while, but it is more likely that you will dismiss it due to its implications concerning your worldview rather than from its apparent improbability alone. Alternative explanations of the events of 9/11 unavoidably accuse other parties, including the media, of unthinkable acts. It would be more logical and more comfortable to not look any further.

Also, as we have become more settled in our own understanding of these events it has become more difficult to consider an opposing explanation (*Source of Bias #2: Unwillingness to look closer*). Just as Jack and Lenny put up blinders because they were so convinced that they couldn't be wrong, we too have fallen into our conceptual ruts around 9/11. These conceptual ruts are our biases, and we most definitely have them about 9/11.

Our relationship with 9/11 can also offer important insight into the topic of Central Banking. Are the Central Banks behind a century or more of military conflict? It is entirely possible but only if you are willing to challenge widely held narratives and accept that one of the pillars of our democracy, a free press, has become a tool of unseen power brokers or something else. Just like Central Banking, 9/11 is less about identifying and bringing justice to the "true" perpetrators than it is about conducting an honest examination of the media. As we concluded in the last chapter, we can all accept the fact that different media sources report "the news" differently but here we are talking about the possibility of a long history of deliberate suppression of information that would irrevocably change the way we view ourselves and our history as a species. I would like to address the 9/11 topic with this mind.

Has our press accurately and responsibly informed the public about what transpired on 9/11? Have they endeavored to objectively articulate all or even some of the contradictory points of view concerning this event? The only way to answer these questions is to drop the "media filter" and go directly to the source of these disputes: the 9/11 Commission report and the supporting technical discussion provided by the National Institute for Standards and Technology (NIST). This chapter is devoted to a direct examination of the "official story" so that we can each come to our own conclusions *about the media* and whether it is worthy of the trust we place in it.

I contend that this kind of "deep dive" is long overdue. Consider the fact that there is one position listed above that applies to the tiniest of minorities, if anyone at all. This is the last one. If you have actually read the extensive technical discussion NIST has offered (this is where the official explanation of how and why the buildings fell is explained) in its entirety, it is very possible that you stand alone. The vast majority of us have formed our opinion about 9/11 *without ever having read the official report* or considered the methodology behind their investigation.

9/11 Commission

The 9/11 Commission was organized by the Bush Administration in response to the pressure placed upon it by the families of the 9/11 victims and the concerned public to explain why and how the buildings came down. The 9/11 events also represented the three biggest structural failures in modern history. Because this also directly impacts public safety, the 9/11 Commission tasked the National Institute for Standards and Technology (NIST), a branch of the Department of Commerce, to perform a technical investigation into the cause and mechanism of the failures. NIST is a body of engineers, scientists and applied mathematicians that are responsible for establishing and enforcing standards for industry in the interest of public safety. NIST was responsible for explaining why and how the twin towers and World Trade Center Building 7 were destroyed on September 11, 2001. It is their report which stands as the "official" explanation that we will be examining.

As mentioned above, few have actually read the thousands of pages of the body of the report and the numerous technical attachments provided by the National Institute for Standards and Technology (NIST). Most people believe that NIST explains how those three buildings came down. *It does not.* Instead it attempts to explain how those three buildings *could* have come down *from plane strikes and (or in the case of Bldg 7, only) office fires.* This may seem like a minor technicality, but it is in fact a major oversight. The investigation *presupposes* that the planes and/or fires were the *only* cause and disregards the possibility of other causes. Every possibility was not considered. In fact, only one was.

Prior to September 11, 2001 a steel-framed building had *never* collapsed from any event **except a planned demolition**. Why didn't the official explanation explore this possibility as well? For some people this may seem like an inflammatory attack on the official report. After all, millions of people watched the planes hit the buildings on TV. Why should any other explanation be entertained? To a scientist, or any organization interested in due diligence (e.g. NIST), it is grossly negligent to not explore all conceivable possibilities before arriving at any conclusion. Even an eleventh grade chemistry student must address other possibilities that may explain the results of their experiment in their lab report. The fact that planes struck buildings in Manhattan is indisputable, but can we be *certain* that there was not another mechanism in play?

Putting all geo-political ideology aside, we must agree that a diligent, scientific approach to understanding the structural failures of these massive buildings is required in the interest of public safety alone. On 9/11 our world suffered the three biggest structural failures in the history of modern skyscraper design and yet only one hypothesis was ever considered. As we diligently examine NIST's explanations and reexamine what we have been told we will each likely end up with different opinions from each other. The information I will present is detailed, technical and provocative. The most important question to keep in mind throughout this critique of the official investigation is *why NIST chose not to explore any other possibilities.* This is the loose thread that begs a tug.

There are two ways to challenge a hypothesis. One is to offer a different one that is as plausible or more plausible. Many dissenters, in this case a group I will call "9/11 Truthers," believe that an alternative explanation, controlled demolition (the detonation of strategically placed explosives), has either been proven or is at least far more likely than a gravitational collapse. To reach this conclusion ultimately requires you to place your faith in the opinion or findings of third parties. For this reason I will exclude any discussion of this approach initially.

The other way to challenge a hypothesis is to find any assumptions that were made that must necessarily be true and demonstrate these assumptions to be false. Recall that NIST did not explain how and why the buildings fell, they only attempted to explain how the Twin Towers *might* have fallen from plane strikes and office fires. Is there anything required of their explanation that is impossible? I will address this question in depth below. Before doing so it is sensible to first qualify what I mean by "impossible". As history has demonstrated, what was once thought to be impossible is often eventually proven possible as our understanding of nature evolves. For the purposes of discussion, impossible will mean what is not possible given our *present* understanding of the Laws of Nature. Recall that in science Laws are the foundation of our model of scientific reality. That is the best we can ever do.

A. Where did the Buildings go?

Each of the Twin Towers was 110 stories, about 1300 feet tall. At the end of the collapse of each one there was a pile of rubble and steel on the ground that was on average 1-2 stories tall. In other words, the pile of debris from a 110 story building made from hundreds of thousands of tons of steel and concrete, its contents of office furniture, electrical generators, HVAC components and plumbing was reduced to a pile 2% of its height with most of it stacked up in the buildings' footprint. Proportionally, if a ten story building falling upon itself did the same thing it would leave a pile about *2 feet high*. The question is, what happened to all the building material and its contents?

Many people who had access to ground zero immediately after the attack, including George Pataki, then Governor of NY, were struggling with the same question. The Governor appeared on CNN[5] several days after 9/11 and (at 2:08 in the clip) was clearly mystified at the absence of concrete at the base of the building. He plainly stated that lower Manhattan was covered with 1-3 inches of *pulverized concrete dust*. There were hardly any blocks of concrete to be found. We can understand how any structure can fall; even a steel structure can be brought down if key components of its structural integrity were compromised. The building would presumably lean to one side or another and come crashing down upon adjoining buildings leaving enormous piles of twisted girders and material everywhere. *That is not what happened to the twin towers*. They fell straight down leaving relatively little material at their base.

Imagine a wrecking ball knocking a building apart. Swinging a wrecking ball back and forth until a building is leveled takes a lot of energy. How much energy would be required to not just knock the twin towers down but to crush *all the concrete in the buildings to dust*? NIST's explanation proposes that no added energy was needed to bring the buildings down and pulverize the concrete and dismember its steel. They posit that gravity alone caused each twin tower not just to fall but to *crush itself*. We can all imagine a building falling down, but crushing *itself entirely*? It would be **impossible** to construct a building that could pulverize *all* of its concrete and rip apart *all* of its steel from its own weight. Remember, we are not talking about a building that came apart leaving large portions intact; most of the twin towers disintegrated. Of course, if enough energy is imparted to building materials they can be reduced to dust, but should we expect that a building can do that to itself? How could such a structure stand to begin with?

The twin towers had been standing for thirty years. Of course *something* could knock them over, but why would we accept that on that particular day they were heavy enough to pulverize the very concrete they were made from into billowing clouds of dust that spread over lower Manhattan?

If you are not careful your mind will rationalize that this could indeed happen because the buildings were "extremely heavy". NIST in fact refers to "the enormous weight" of the top portions of the buildings crushing the bottom portions through a collapse sequence that was "inevitable" once the supporting columns and lateral trusses were weakened. NIST, however, suspiciously omits any discussion of the behavior of the building during the collapse in their discussion.

The top portions of the building were indeed "heavy" but heavy compared to what? By suggesting that their weight was enough to crush the bottom portions of the building within a few seconds, how then can one explain why the building could stand in the first place? The vast majority of the steel skeleton of the building was undamaged from the plane strikes. Why would it break apart suddenly and uniformly from a weight it was designed to hold indefinitely? It is easy to succumb to *Source of Bias #7 (Misunderstanding the pertinence of the evidence)* because we tend to regard skyscrapers as very big things that could crush anything in their path. They could indeed crush many things, but does it make sense that they could do that to *themselves?* It is understandable if you are uncertain about this. It is possible that your uncertainty stems from *Source of Bias #3 (Unbalanced inquiry).* Most of us have never taken a hard look at what the official explanation contends. Below we will explore the scientific basis by which we can confidently dismiss the possibility that a building could pulverize itself from its own weight.

First, consider a different situation. Imagine a very tall stack of bricks. There is a limit to how many bricks can be stacked one atop another because at some point the weight on the bottom brick will be enough to crush it. In engineering terms, the *compressive strength* of the brick on the bottom will be exceeded if the stack is too tall. Let us say that the bricks are stacked as high as they possibly could be without crushing the bottom brick. We then strike the stack near its top hard enough to damage some of the bricks or even displace them out of the stack. We can all imagine the bricks ending up in a pile on the ground. Why would we predict that they would *all* end up crushed into a pile of dust? If the *bottom* brick was able to withstand all of the weight upon it before we destabilized the stack, why would the *entire* stack, including the ones at the top, be pulverized by its own weight? That would be impossible. Note that we could use any material we wished in this example from bricks to bars of soap to hollow blocks of balsa wood. The only difference would be in the maximum height of the initial stack of material. In every case we would expect they would fall into a pile of objects, not a pile of pulverized material.

NIST does not address this conundrum directly but simply states that it *must* be possible because that is what we "observed". This is a reasonable conclusion but *only if no other explanations are considered*. In fact, even if we choose to ignore other possible mechanisms of collapse this theory requires another impossibility to work. In order for the top portion of the building to crush the lower *it must be stronger than the lower portion*.

Take a simpler example involving bricks again. Let us say that you needed to crush a single brick into dust. The only tool that you have available is a pickaxe. Would it work? Maybe. But what if the pickaxe itself was made of brick too? Every time you struck the brick hard enough to make it crumble the axe would necessarily break apart as well.

In physics this is described by Newton's Third Law of Motion, which dictates that objects acting upon each other must be subject to equal and opposite forces from each other. By proposing that the upper portion of the building (approximately 12 floors in the North Tower for example) could completely crush the lower portion (98 floors) while remaining intact we are introducing another impossibility. The upper and lower portions of the building were made of the *same* stuff! In fact, the upper portions of the building were lighter and less sturdy than the lower portions because they were designed to hold up less weight. If the upper portion was in fact crushing the lower portion *why isn't it getting crushed itself*? Newton's third law dictates that whatever force the upper portion is imparting upon the lower *must be imparted to the upper portion as well*. Getting the top to drive itself through a more heavily designed structure by dismembering and pulverizing it on its way down while remaining intact itself is **impossible**. Once again it is Sir Isaac Newton's musings that invite us to reconsider another seemingly open and shut case.

B. Speed of Collapse of the Twin Towers

Calculations have been made about how much energy it would take to pulverize all of the concrete in the buildings and it turns out that it is more than twice as much as the gravitational potential energy of the standing building. In other words, even if all the energy of the falling building was converted into crushing the concrete and dismembering its steel frame there would still be a large deficit of energy. For the purposes of this discussion, forget about the calculations. If we are interested in clarifying our own understanding of this event it is important to exclude third-party opinions and calculations. Let us say that the weight of the building could pulverize itself. That is already impossible as was mentioned above. If we suspend rationality and continue with NIST's logic yet another impossibility arises.

If the concrete is being pulverized, energy is being expended. The only source of energy in the official explanation is the kinetic energy of the upper part of the buildings. Kinetic energy is the energy possessed by a body in motion, in this case, the upper part of the building which was put in motion by gravity. If the kinetic energy is being used to pulverize the concrete, *the fall of the building should have been slowed.* Both twin towers fell at approximately 6.3 meters per second squared, or approximately two-thirds the acceleration of gravity. If that doesn't make sense to you, look at any video of the collapses. The top of the building is *accelerating* towards the ground at more than 64% of free-fall. If a piece of concrete had been thrown off the top of the tower as it began to fall it would have hit the ground just two seconds before the top of the building did. It would have barely beaten hundreds of thousands of tons of reinforced steel and concrete designed to do one thing: remain standing while supporting the structure above it.

The towers, like all modern buildings, were built to exacting standards which demanded three to five times the strength to hold up the building. This is an extremely large safety tolerance, yet we watched them crumble to the ground under their own weight. It would have been **impossible** for such an over-designed structure to fall that fast through the path of greatest resistance from gravity alone. Each tower took about 12 seconds to fall. On average, 9 floors *per second* are being destroyed. Indeed, because the top of the building is accelerating towards the ground, each of the bottom floors are disintegrating in less than a *twentieth of a second.*

There is no denying the buildings came down quickly. We have ample, undisputed footage of both collapses. But are we observing buildings crushing themselves or are we actually watching buildings fall because the very material from which they are constructed is being destroyed by another source of energy? Is it possible to know? It is.

The buildings are falling at rates that dictate that the concrete and steel are putting up a fraction of the resistance they were designed to provide. If they are not putting up resistance they shouldn't be getting blown to bits. This is a very important concept to understand. In order for the materials to get destroyed, they must have absorbed the energy of the fall. If they absorbed the energy of the fall, the rate of collapse should have been much slower. How much slower? It is a function of how strong the structure is relative to the weight it is supporting. In this case, we are talking about free-standing structures designed to hold their structural loads with huge safety tolerances. Remember, the buildings did not end up in a pile of large concrete blocks and twisted girders. The materials were decimated. Basic laws of motion dictate that if gravity is the only source of energy involved either a rapid fall will result, leaving large blocks of concrete and intact steel or that a slow or partial collapse will result, leaving materials that get destroyed in their entirety. We cannot have a rapid fall *and* pulverized concrete and dismembered steel--if gravity alone were in play.

Consider this example to illustrate. We have all seen a karate expert break wooden boards held by an assistant with their fist. In order for the boards to break the expert's fist must be moving with sufficient speed. But what if the assistant fails to hold the boards in place and allows them to recoil from impact? The boards will not break. It does not matter how fast the expert's fist is moving, broken boards will only result if they *absorb* the energy of his fist.

We must conclude that the integrity of the materials must have been or *were being* compromised at the time of collapse. There was not any "crushing" going on. We have been in fact watching buildings falling because the very materials holding them up are being synchronously pulverized and ripped apart by a source of energy not acknowledged by NIST but *clearly present*. You cannot "see" energy, you can only infer its existence by the behavior of the system you are examining. The behavior of the buildings as they fell proves that there was another massive source of energy at work. Collapses with the rapidity that we witnessed, leaving only pulverized concrete and dismembered steel, would have been **impossible** from gravity alone.

Perhaps you are one of the many people who happened to tune into the live TV coverage of what was unfolding in Manhattan before the twin towers collapsed. I tuned in soon after the second tower was struck. Just like millions of other viewers I and those with me were shocked at what was transpiring. Our shock turned to disbelief when the first of the twin towers fell to the ground. Everyone in the room was struck with a wordless surprise, a sense that something didn't make sense, that what was happening shouldn't be happening. It seemed that the buildings were being crushed like soda cans under the heel of an enormous boot or a giant hammer--but there weren't any boots or hammers. These steel structures were instead behaving like towers built from playing cards, barely able to stand on their own. Moreover the "cards" did not end up in a pile on the ground. They were shredded into tiny pieces as they fell.

Our intuition about this would not have been wrong; in fact what is offered above is the technical explanation that supports what our intuition was telling us at that moment. Only later, after the media endlessly confirmed that the only possible explanation were the plane strikes were people able to dismiss their mute puzzlement about what they witnessed. Because no other explanation was offered, the public didn't have a choice. If you are curious, get a group of 11 year old kids together and let them watch a 12 second clip of the North Tower "collapsing" (["Collapse" of North Tower](6)) and ask them if it is falling down or blowing up. You may be surprised at what an unbiased set of eyes will see. This slow motion clip is narrated by David Chandler, a professor of physics. I suggest that you observe the video in silence without listening to his commentary in order to avoid introducing any bias into your opinion. The intent here is to examine the details of what is in front of our eyes without third party validation.

C. Lateral expulsion of material and Human Remains

It is well documented that many four and eight ton steel frame members were thrown 600 feet away from each of the Twin Towers at speeds clocked by physicists of 80 mph. Imagine the amount of energy required to rip eight tons of steel from a building and send it hurtling off as fast as a speeding car on a highway. Gravity works in only one direction. If the only force acting on the building was straight down it is **impossible** for structural members to be thrown at such velocity perpendicular to the force. This necessitates the presence of an explosive, or expulsive, force *perpendicular* to the force of gravity. It is important to note that these structural elements did not hit the ground and scatter. They were jettisoned from the building as it fell, lodging themselves in the upper floors of nearby buildings.

Steel and concrete were not the only things thrown from the buildings. During the painstaking search for survivors and human remains the FDNY and dedicated members of the NY Medical Examiner's office were startled to find bits and pieces of human beings far from the building. These discoveries received little attention at the time but reentered the public's view years later when a proposal to construct an Islamic center near the WTC site drew criticism from people who felt that a building with such symbolic undertones needed to be built further away from the site out of respect for the innocent victims of the tragedy. But how far was far enough? The next block? Ground Zero was not just a point on the ground the protesters argued, it was an area of considerable size, an area at least as big as the territory across which victims were found. Here we have a map[7] of lower Manhattan where the FDNY labeled all the spots where human remains from the towers' destruction were found. Parts of victims bodies were strewn over a large area surrounding the center of the WTC complex. Hundreds of separate pieces of human tissue were found hundreds of yards away. One piece of remains was found 1,135 feet from Ground Zero. Does it make sense that the bodies of people trapped in the building could be thrown *nearly ¼ of a mile away* if it fell from gravity alone?

In this article[8] from the NY Times Dr. Charles S. Hirch, chief medical examiner of NY at the time of 9/11 describes the unique challenge of confirming the identity of victims of this disaster. No traces of many of the victims were ever found. Only solitary fragments of bones of others were identified. Even more disturbing was the fact that one victim's body was divided into *200 separate pieces.*

What are we to conclude from this confirmed evidence? Obviously the death toll from these collapses were tragically high, but what kind of injuries would we have suspected as the result of a building collapse? Clearly there would be a lot of dismemberment and crush injuries but what kind of mechanism could cause a human body to disintegrate into two hundred pieces or throw other body parts over a thousand feet away? This combined with multi-ton structural components ejected to a distance of two football fields makes an explosive event a much more likely mechanism behind the destruction of these buildings. Yet evidence of explosions were never explored in the official investigation. Later in this chapter we will examine possible reasons behind this lack of diligence.

D. Fires at Ground Zero

It took *three months* to put the fires out at the World Trade Center. It was reported that the FDNY flooded ground zero with four million gallons of water, completely submerging the basement fires. Ground zero was covered with water for months. Fire can only exist if an oxygen source is present. We have been given the explanation that the fires continued to burn because the steel was subjected to a significant amount of friction from the collapse which created a tremendous amount of heat. Because the metal was so hot fires reignited when debris was intermittently cleared allowing oxygen to reenter. Let us examine this hypothesis more closely:

First, the fact that the steel girders were so hot is not proof that friction was the only cause of the heat, it is only an observation that the hypothesis seeks to explain. Next, we can all agree that although fires were burning in a limited part of the buildings while they were still standing, most of the steel was at room temperature moments before the beginning of the collapse. If the driving force behind the collapse was gravity alone, as the official explanation argues, why would the steel become so hot? Of course there would be an increase in temperature as the kinetic energy of the buildings' fall distorted the steel, but would it have brought it close to its melting point? We can shrug our shoulders and say that it is possible, but is it likely? We are not all material scientists or chemists but what do we know from our basic understanding of how we work with steel? In order to get steel hot enough that it can be poured into molds or made responsive to a blacksmith's hammer it takes time in sophisticated furnaces or crucibles. Here we are talking about collapse sequences that took only about 11 seconds. Once they hit the ground, no more energy was being transferred to the steel. It is nonsensical to think that exposure to friction for 11 seconds can render so much steel so hot.

Next let us look at the concept of "friction". Friction is a force that opposes motion and in doing so converts the energy of movement into heat. If there was a lot of friction present during the fall of the buildings *why did they fall so fast*? The twin towers fell at nearly two thirds the rate of gravity. This is demonstrative of collapses that were met with little resistance at all. If anything it points to conspicuous **lack** of friction.

Water is one of the quickest ways to cool steel. Using water to cool recently molded steel items runs the risk of decreasing the strength of the steel *because* it cools it so fast. When very hot metal is submerged, the water in contact with the steel will evaporate very quickly and be released, exposing the steel to more water. The more water that evaporates, the more heat is being transferred away from the steel. The faster the water evaporates, the quicker the steel cools. Because ground-zero was underwater the steel must have been in contact with the water most of the time getting cooler and cooler by the second. Does it seem plausible that steel exposed to heat for just 11 seconds would take months to cool underwater? It is far more likely if not certain that there was another source of energy contributing to the heat of the steel *while it was submerged*.

Finally we get to the last part of the hypothesis: the steel and debris was set ablaze intermittently whenever air was introduced as the area was exhumed. This is why, we are told, the fires continued to burn for months despite all the water upon them. It is true that if enough heat is present fires will absolutely reignite when oxygen is provided and be extinguished when oxygen is removed. The mystery here is how oxygen can be introduced *if the whole area was underwater.* If air can get there so too can water. Water, being more dense than air, will immediately displace it.

I am not suggesting the fires were not burning for three months (CNN [9]); I am only pointing out the basic truth that the only way fires can burn underwater or remain so hot for so long is through a *chemical* reaction that has an oxygen molecule as a reactant. There must have been an oxygen source *in or on the material that was burning.* This would have allowed the fires to continue whether or not water or oxygen was introduced.

E. The Collapse of WTC BUILDING 7

Finally, there is the problem with building 7, the building referenced earlier. It was a modern steel structured skyscraper 47 stories tall that suffered isolated fires on several floors. It was **not** hit by a plane.

Even today many Americans do not know that a *third* building was destroyed on 9/11. It occurred about seven hours after the second twin tower was destroyed. Building 7 fell in under 7 seconds. As you can observe here[10] the building fell uniformly through the path of (what should have been the) greatest resistance into its own footprint. Unlike the twin towers, this building fell at or very near free-fall. If you were standing on its rooftop when it started to collapse you would have hit the ground at the same time if you jumped off the building. This means that not a single one of the 80 columns in the building offered any resistance to the fall. Once again, if the structure put up no resistance to the fall, why did the columns get crushed? NIST took *seven years* to come up with their analysis of the fall of Building 7.

The best way to investigate how a complex structure like a building will behave when subjected to damage would be to use a computer model. The model can be adjusted by changing the parameters of the strength of the steel, the weight of the concrete, the temperature of the fires, etc. and then observing how the model behaves. This is in fact what NIST did. They used computer simulations to attempt to prove their hypothesis that building 7's collapse was caused by the failure of a single column from isolated fires. No matter how much they adjusted their model, they could not get it to fall in the way we observed. *Using their own computer model,* **NIST has** *disproven their own hypothesis.* Why then would they officially "conclude" that it was the failure of a single column (Column 79 on the 12th floor) that resulted in the global collapse of this building?

An isolated column failure cannot cause a steel building to fall at free-fall acceleration - or symmetrically. That is *impossible.* If a new, four hundred foot wide, 47 seven story building can fall at the speed of gravity through its own supporting columns from the failure of a single column on just one floor, why do demolition teams need to painstakingly set up hundreds of explosive charges on multiple floors to demolish old buildings? NIST spent seven years trying to explain what happened and couldn't. Though they *claim* that they have adequately explained the collapse with their model in their official statement, their computer simulation does not approach what we observed. They haven't proved their hypothesis correct. They have in fact proved their hypothesis wrong. This is indisputable. Why didn't they look for another explanation after their model failed to confirm their hypothesis? What exactly was their mandate? More importantly, why didn't our media point out this glaring failure in due diligence and inexplicable lapse of basic logic?

The reality is that many teams of engineers and architects, academic and private, have openly questioned NIST's analysis and conclusions. Requests for correction have been repeatedly submitted and ignored. Furthermore, when NIST was requested to provide the parameters they used to simulate their model they refused, citing the need to keep them from the public in the interest of National Security. As of this year (2020), at least one independent study[11], conducted by the University of Alaska, has proven that building 7 could not have come down in the manner which we witnessed from fires alone. If you are unaware of this study, why is that?

Although I have directed the discussion to pointing out the inconsistencies of the official explanation, the real matter of interest here is not in picking sides or in proving or disproving the findings of the "experts". It is about our media's coverage of such heated disputes between such authorities. Does it make sense that no mainstream media source has ever acknowledged that there is strong and organized opposition to the official conclusions and methodology from experts in the field? How are we to interpret the reality that this opposing position has instead been endlessly and ruthlessly characterized as a fringe movement held by irrational people with ulterior motives?

The fate of Building 7 is particularly important. If you weren't aware of the destruction of building 7 you wouldn't have been alone. Why is that? Why did this event get so little coverage in the media? How do you interpret the fact that four planes were hijacked and four buildings were either completely destroyed (the twin towers and building 7) or damaged (The Pentagon) yet only *three* buildings suffered plane collisions? Is it possible that the media have not been honest, objective or at the very least thorough?

If these impossibilities were not enough, there are also a number of amazing coincidences that occurred that morning.

F. Shanksville, PA

United Airlines flight 93 was the fourth plane that was hijacked that morning. It never struck a building like the other three. It crashed into a grassy field in rural Pennsylvania. The reports surrounding the event are surprisingly murky. The official report states that much of the plane and its passengers *disintegrated* on impact. We cannot say that this is impossible, we can only say that this has never happened before. Unless a plane ends up at the bottom of an ocean, plane crashes leave debris fields and passenger remains that can be analyzed. Relatively very little was found at the site, yet this plane crashed into a field on American soil on a sunny Tuesday morning. The coroner claims that only bits and fragments of human remains were found. There was no fuselage or luggage and very little of the massive jet engines. These are the most rugged portions of the plane and its contents. Clearly this is indicative of an astounding amount of impact energy that we cannot dismiss as an impossibility in a jet plane crash. However, two Saudi Passports managed to escape unharmed. How probable is this? Does it seem improbable enough to warrant further investigation by the media?

This story brings up another glaring inconsistency with the official explanation. Two planes can tear through steel and concrete yet this one disintegrates after striking dirt?

G. Cell phone calls from the Passengers

The 911 Commission report states that over a dozen cellular phone calls were made from passengers in the planes that were hijacked that morning. Time logs indicate that the calls were made while the planes were in flight. The recordings of the passengers can be heard. The passengers clearly state the planes have been hijacked. They sound distracted but calm. One caller states that the hijackers appear to be of "middle eastern descent". Several of the calls lasted more than a minute. Is it possible that the hijackers would have permitted those calls? Absolutely. It is also possible that the calls were made quietly without their knowledge.

The problem with the story is that some of these calls were made on personal cellular phones while in flight. This is nearly impossible today, nineteen years later. The idea that this could have been possible in 2001 is difficult to accept. Cell phone towers are designed to detect and transmit signals laterally, not upward and downward. Even if a connection could have been made momentarily the tower would have had to immediately hand the signal over to another station rapidly due to the speed of the plane. There were no breaks in coverage on the recordings. As of this year, 2020, I have not been able to get consistent cellular phone coverage on a plane flying at more than a few thousand feet of altitude using a direct phone to tower (not a plane wifi) connection.

What does this mean? One cannot definitively know; one can only conjecture. It is only offered here as another glaring inconsistency of the official explanation. What would be the benefit of including this in the official report? Why were there so few questions asked about the credibility of maintaining clear, uninterrupted cellular phone calls made on flip-phones in 2001 from planes flying at elevation?

H. NORAD exercises

It is customary for NORAD (the North American Aerospace Defense Command) to deploy fighter jets when an airline hijacking is in progress. No fighter pilot ever made visual contact with any of the planes that were hijacked on 9/11. There have been some explanations for this including the fact that the airliners' transponders were turned off by the hijackers and couldn't be tracked. What is not as generally known is that very few fighter jets were scrambled that morning. Most of our Air Defense system was engaged in flight exercises over the midwest and Canada that very morning. Operation Vigilant Guardian (among others) was a live exercise involving fighter squadrons and military bases that was conducted on the morning of September 11, 2001. The terrorists happened to have picked the very morning that most of our assets were unavailable to protect even the most heavily defended building on Earth, the Pentagon.

How are we to know that these exercises actually took place? Several years after 9/11, Georgia Representative Cynthia McKinney directly questioned then Secretary of Defense Donald Rumsfeld and General Richard Meyers (Joint Chiefs of Staff Chairman) regarding this exercise. At this hearing General Meyers confirms at approximately 7 minutes into this clip[12] that in fact four exercises involving our air defenses were happening while the hijacked planes headed to their targets. Moreover he reveals to us that the exercises were *designed to simulate hijacked planes being used as weapons to fly into buildings.* We can only imagine the confusion that resulted on the ground when four actual hijackings were occurring simultaneously with simulated ones.

Is it possible that the terrorists knew about this opening in our air defenses? Yes. Is it possible that they just got extremely lucky with the timing? Yes. Neither of these possibilities can be deemed impossible. It is the *improbability* of this "coincidence" that is striking. Certainly it would be worthy of an investigative report by our media, yet none ever came.

I. Twin Tower Collapse Sequence

NIST does not explain definitively how either twin tower fell so quickly. They propose a possible explanation involving trusses weakened by jet fuel and office fires that eventually sagged and gave way, allowing the concrete floors they supported to fall but more importantly causing the peripheral columns to bend inward allowing the upper sections of the building to fall upon the lower. The calculations which should use the strength of the columns and estimated weight of the building to determine if such a collapse is even possible *are not given.* Instead NIST references a research paper that was written just **48 hours after 9/11** by an engineering professor (Zdenek P. **Bažant**) from Northwestern University and one of his students:

"Why did the World Trade Center collapse? A simple analysis"[13]

In this paper the two authors propose a mechanism that they believe could explain a progressive collapse. If you choose to examine it you will find it to be a technical paper and largely uninterpretable unless you are a mechanical engineer. However, there are a few points that the curious among us will find unmistakably puzzling. First is that on page 4 the authors state:

> "The energy dissipation, particularly that due to the inelastic deformation of columns during the initial drop of the upper part, *may be neglected*, i.e., the upper part may be assumed to move through distance h almost *in a free fall ...*"

This assumption should strike you as mysterious. The authors are assuming that when the top of the building began to collapse *all* of the columns on the damaged floors failed *completely* and *at exactly the same instant*. Why would they make that assumption and what does it matter? Because it has a direct bearing on what would happen next. They are trying to prove that when the tower began to fall the top of the building was falling fast enough to crush the rest of the building below it. Whether or not this is true cannot be known by you nor I without trusting another's opinion, but does it make sense that *every single steel* column (287 in all) would suddenly give way at precisely the same moment and offer absolutely no resistance to a fall? This assumption is the basis of their argument. The more support the columns offered, the slower the top of the building was falling. Dr. Bazant believes that it is sensible to think that none of the columns offered any support.

The other important value that can be readily interpreted by the lay reader is the estimate of the weight of the upper portion of the building. Obviously the greater that weight, the greater the chance of a collapse. From the paper:

> "...mass of the upper part (of North Tower) $\approx 58 \cdot 10^6$ kg"

Dr. Bazant estimates its weight to be about 58 million kilograms or about 64 thousand tons. You don't need to be an engineer or an architect or a physics professor to recognize that this number is absolutely crucial in determining whether or not the building could have suffered an unstoppable collapse from gravity alone. How are we to know what the actual weight of the upper portions of the buildings were? We must concede that we, the public, cannot know without trusting another source. However shouldn't we expect that NIST would, at the very least, demand that this crucial value be consistent with their *own* estimates? They did not.

In fact, Dr. Bazant nearly *doubles the weight of the upper portion of the building compared to **NIST's estimates**.* NIST's estimate of the weight of the top part of the North Tower can be found here [14] in *NCSTAR 1-6D : Global Structural Analysis of the World Trade Center Towers to Impact Damage and Fire.* In this official document on page 176 in table 4-7 are NIST's estimates of the structural load carried by the peripheral and central columns at floor 98. All summed it equals approximately 73,000 kilo-pounds (kips) or 33 million kilograms... 44% *less* than the number in Dr. Bazant's analysis.

If you were curious enough to check the reference to *NCSTAR 1-6D* above you would have seen that the weight of the top section of the building is not explicitly given. Instead, you must find the row of numbers that quantify the structural load on all five sections of columns at floor 98 and add them together. Perhaps this strikes you as somewhat odd that this number, which is so central to a seven year long investigation into the greatest and most perplexing structural failure in modern history, is only indirectly given as a series of numbers embedded in a table in thousands of pages of documents. The fact of the matter is that this is the only reference to this number in all of NIST's analysis. Why? *Because NIST never did any of the analysis themselves.* Their entire position is based on someone else's independent conclusions. That person (Dr. Bazant) did not even use the same number in his calculations and was able to arrive at a complete analysis two days after 9/11.

In other words, if you use NIST's own estimate of the weight of the building in the model they reference, a progressive and complete collapse would not be as likely or even possible at all. NIST did not verify this professor's calculations but merely stated that because another party claims it to be possible it must be so. As astonishing as it seems, this internally inconsistent approach continues to stand as the official, "scientific" explanation of the incredible mystery we all witnessed when the twin towers unexpectedly fell to the ground.

Where exactly did Bazant get his estimate? Instead of using the actual weight he decided to use the maximum design load of the columns. In other words, he took the liberty of exaggerating the weight to the maximum weight the structure was designed to safely support. There is no reason to do this other than to skew the calculations to a desired result. This is frank manipulation of data and NIST has been complicit in it.

If you believe we are being unreasonably fastidious about the numbers, put them aside for a moment and examine their approach from a different angle. NIST represents a body of engineers, scientists and applied mathematicians that are arguably the best in the business. They have been educated at the finest institutions and literally set the standards for applied sciences. Why didn't they delegate the calculation of the behavior of the twin towers during their collapse to a team of their own? Explaining the mysterious and sudden collapse of both twin towers into their own footprints was their central directive and should have been the biggest question in their minds. Why would the appointed experts, with complete access to all the technical information of the buildings choose not to look at it themselves and instead defer to a single outsider's opinion? It is completely nonsensical, unless they never had a choice in the matter. Were they specifically directed away from doing the required calculations? If so, why? Given the absurd assumptions Bazant made and his disingenuous use of data we should suspect that no technical authority at NIST would have ever put their name on such an analysis. Having an outsider do the calculation conveniently allows NIST to maintain their technical integrity while not being directly responsible for spurious conclusions. Of course there is no proof of this potential maneuver. We are simply pulling at the loose threads in front of us to try to make sense of an inexplicable lapse in scientific diligence from the authority on scientific diligence itself.

Obviously we, the public, cannot be expected to examine thousands of pages of technical data and dissect the arguments surrounding them, but shouldn't the independent experts in this field have spoken out? They did, but few were *listening*. This glaring omission of accuracy was initially the source of skepticism in the scientific community. Later an article in the magazine Popular Mechanics was published to explain a possible collapse sequence. A similar explanation appeared in a documentary on NOVA. What most people do not realize is that the Popular Mechanics article and the documentary *do not* reflect NIST's official explanation at all. The Popular Mechanics article and the NOVA documentary both attribute the collapse to "pancaking" floors, falling one upon another. They both suggest how one floor falling upon another could *hypothetically* cause a chain reaction resulting in the separation of the floors from the columns, yet neither addresses how the central and peripheral columns, the steel skeleton that supported the building could have been destroyed themselves.

These simplistic explanations also fail to explain how concrete floors can create a "pancaking" collapse while *at the same time be blown out of the building creating huge clouds of pulverized material*. Today many of us continue to picture a stack of floors falling upon a single floor high up in the tower, dismantling it from its supporting trusses and slowly speeding up as each successive floor adds to the momentum of the falling mass while remaining completely intact on its way down. Once the first floor goes, we have been told, the rest is history because now the falling weight is even larger. However, it is clear from every video of the destruction of the two towers that all the concrete is blowing out in huge clouds *as the top of the building is descending*. We also have the physical evidence of pulverized concrete blanketing lower Manhattan. If all the material is being blown outwardly, *what then is doing the crushing*? Once again observe the collapse of the North Tower here.[15] Is there an intact upper portion crushing the rest of the building? **There is not**. Look for yourself. These popularly cited explanations are markedly incomplete and do not actually reflect or support the official explanation, yet they live on in people's minds as a sufficient representation of what happened. Was it too much to ask of an objective observer, trained in hearing all sides of an argument (e.g. a journalist) to ask of NIST, "Excuse me but where exactly is the top section of the building that is supposed to be crushing the bottom part?"

NIST and the research paper above explain that the collapse of each twin tower was initiated on the floors that were struck by the planes. The columns on these floors failed, they hypothesize, because the weight of the upper portion of the building exceeded their strength when the lateral trusses that connected the peripheral and central columns sagged from the heat of the office fires burning on those floors. The upper portion dropped on to the lower and the rest is history. NIST claims that the upper portion of the North Tower, having fallen the height of a single floor, had enough momentum to sequentially overcome the next 98 floors of reinforced steel and concrete. From the undisputed video footage it is clearly that the top part was destroyed first and then the bottom part followed. Nevertheless, even if there were a top portion available to do the crushing NIST never considered whether this was mathematically possible. It must have been, they conclude, because the building fell to the ground and thus, they say, the details are not relevant or within the scope of their analysis. A closer examination, for those interested, is given in the paper by Dr. Bazant.

Perhaps this seems reasonable to you, but is it scientific? It is not. Dr. Bazant's explanation, when examined more rigorously, requires a number of highly improbable events to have occurred. First, his model requires that *every single column on the floors damaged by the plane collisions fail completely, simultaneously and synchronously* in order for a collapse to be initiated. Additionally, his model ignores the energy required to bend, buckle and twist the columns as the upper portion begins to "fall" upon the lower. NIST, by supporting Dr. Bazant's model, chooses to assume that these columns effectively vanished. This is the *only way* enough momentum from the falling sections might have been delivered to the lower sections to initiate a potential collapse. Recall as well that Bazant uses an estimated weight of the building that is nearly twice what NIST calculates.

It is very clear from all of the footage of the towers burning before the collapse that the fires were not equally distributed across the damaged floors. Neither were most of the columns on that floor damaged from the impact of the planes. There were 240 peripheral and 47 central columns in each twin tower. Does it seem reasonable that every single one of those 287 columns on that floor would suddenly fail at precisely the same instant without offering an ounce of resistance? If the fires were burning unequally why would all of the columns fail at the same instant? Should this assumption be an integral part of a technical explanation that serves as the basis of an investigation into the greatest structural failure in modern history?

The improbabilities continue to mount as the collapse progresses. In his model, the upper section of each building falls through and annihilates each floor below successively. As it does so, all 287 *columns on each floor also had to have failed at precisely the same instant in exactly the same way.* This is the only way the buildings could have fallen straight down. If any group of columns behaved any differently by remaining intact a little longer or shorter than the rest the collapse would have been asymmetric. Because the collapse was uniform and symmetric we are forced to accept that this could have happened 80 times in a row in the South Tower and then 98 times in a row in the North tower a short while later. In his model, once the upper sections of each building bulldozed their way down miraculously unaffected, they then proceeded to crush themselves when they hit the ground. This is the official explanation.

Interestingly one could look at this entirely differently. Having every single support column fail simultaneously, some suggest, may actually be something common. We would know this, they say, because it happened twice on the same day (tower 2 followed by tower 1). Isn't it more reasonable that it points in exactly the other direction? The fact that something *that* unlikely happened *twice* should essentially assure us that some other mechanism was in play in both instances.

J. Heat of the fires

Much debate has taken place over the temperature of jet fuel and the melting point of steel. It is true that the melting point of steel is significantly higher than the temperature of burning jet fuel (2500 F vs 1500 F). However, supporters of the conventional story maintain that over time, the heat would have weakened the steel to the point of collapse. It is difficult to prove they are wrong. This is often central to the argument of many "debunkers". It has been demonstrated that given enough time, steel weakens near the temperatures of burning jet fuel. However, even if the strength of the steel had been compromised, steel does not fail from heat in the way that Dr. Bazant requires. As steel gets hot and begins to approach its melting point it will begin to bend and distort gradually from the load it is bearing. It does not snap apart instantaneously like a pencil allowing what is above to go into a free fall.

It is also difficult to believe that so much of the fuel would have remained ignited for so long. It is obvious that most of the fuel exploded when the plane struck the building. Huge fireballs erupted which burned a great deal of the fuel at the moment of each plane collision. *NIST itself confirms that most of the fuel erupted at impact and that the fuel that had entered the building had burned completely in the first **ten minutes***. Does it seem reasonable that those massive structures would have entirely collapsed from a ten minute burn? A fully fueled Boeing 767 carries approximately 24,000 gallons of fuel. If half of that fuel spread through a building like one of the twin towers that would equate to about 120 gallons or three barrels per floor. How likely is it that just three barrels of jet fuel burning for ten minutes on concrete floors that are each one *acre* in size would weaken a building to the point where it would fall straight down under its own weight?

Even if much of the fuel did not ignite immediately but found its way inside the twin towers how hot could it have been? Video clearly demonstrates that the smoke billowing from the fires was black, indicating that they were oxygen starved (and thus cooler) for most of the time they were burning. NIST's explanation requires the temperature around the supporting columns to be at or near 1500 degrees where the plane hit in order for the steel trusses to sag and a collapse sequence to begin. If that were the case, how can we explain the unfortunate people in the building that appeared at the periphery on the very floors that were hit waving and exhorting others to help them? If it were 1500 degrees on those floors they would have been incapacitated in a few seconds. The columns *on these specific floors* were required at some point to catastrophically and instantaneously buckle for the collapse to be initiated. It is highly improbable that the steel was as hot as NIST states.

The argument that fires from ignited jet fuel and office furniture also fails to explain the ejection of molten metal from the twin towers after the planes struck and before they fell to the ground. As stated above, the melting point of steel is considerably higher than the temperature of burning jet fuel. If burning jet fuel and office furniture were the only sources of heat it may weaken steel but not liquefy it. Debunkers acknowledge that molten metal was seen coming from several points on the exterior of the twin towers. They attempt to explain this by noting that aluminum melts at about 1200F, less than burning jet fuel. Most claim that what we saw was actually melted portions of the plane dripping out of the building (view it here[16]). You may find it reasonable that the plane's aluminum melted and somehow found its way out of the building a few floors from the impact point. However firefighters unequivocally state that molten *steel* was observed in the basement levels of the twin towers prior to their collapse. Here[17] FDNY Captain Philip Ruvolo surrounded by his team describes that "molten steel was flowing like lava". Does it seem reasonable that the plane melted from fires and found its way to the basement eighty or more floors away creating a scene from a "foundry" or "volcano" as he described in his own words?

Is there another explanation?

Perhaps these points don't make you reconsider the official story. Many cannot look away. If there were no other way to explain these impossibilities it is likely that most "9/11 Truthers" would shrug their shoulders and go with the official explanation. The difficulty is that *there is a simple alternative explanation for all of these impossibilities and inexplicable observations.* We now arrive at the second way of challenging a hypothesis: offering a different one that is *more likely.*

A. What is a "Controlled Demolition?"

Controlled demolition involves rigging a building with charges designed to first cut the supporting columns so that other charges, when detonated, will destabilize the structure. There would have been a lot of cutting charges required to set the building up for a collapse. This would have very likely resulted in a lot of molten steel that would have found its way to the lower floors explaining what the firefighters witnessed at the basement levels. This is precisely how steel framed buildings are demolished. If timed correctly, the building can be blown up from the top down (twin towers) or bottom up (building 7). The collapse will be very fast and sudden. If it is demolished from the bottom up the building will fall at or near the acceleration of gravity (building 7). Depending upon the energy density of the explosive used, concrete will indeed be pulverized and so too can large fragments be thrown laterally.

One explosive that is being suggested as the one that could have been used is nano-thermite. Nano-thermite is a variant of a well-known chemical combination known as thermate (essentially elemental Aluminum and Iron Oxide). When heat is added to these reactants, the oxide molecule leaves the iron and bonds with Aluminum releasing a great deal of energy in the form of heat. Within a few seconds this reaction produces temperatures that exceed 4000 degrees F, easily enough to melt and cut steel. This reaction is impervious to water because the oxygen is provided in the Iron Oxide reactant. It would explain why metal continued to burn for three months despite being doused with water continuously.

Three independent teams have confirmed the presence of nano-thermite in thin red flakes that were found in and near ground zero. How do we know that this material was really found? We cannot *know*, we must *trust* another party, yet this would explain what the conventional narrative cannot. By dismissing independent researchers that claim to have found proof of explosive material we are, by default, *trusting* NIST and their opinion that searching for such evidence was unnecessary. However if we accept that material was actually found we arrive at an explanation of what we are observing: a massive source of unexplained energy, lateral expulsion of materials, pulverized concrete, dismembered steel, chemical reactions that took months to complete and a coherent model of what happened that day.

B. Witnesses to Explosions

Interestingly, NIST addressed the possibility of a controlled demolition in just one paragraph of thousands of pages of technical explanations and discussion. They decided *not* to investigate that possibility because, they claimed, no explosions were ever witnessed. Yet there are numerous accounts from first responders unequivocally stating that they witnessed explosions in the buildings. We know this because Thomas Von Essen, the city fire commissioner on Sept. 11, had ordered the gathering and archiving of oral testimony from 503 first responders. These 12000 pages of first hand accounts taken between October, 2001 and January, 2002 were released to the public in response to a lawsuit filed by the NY Times and families of some of the victims of 9/11. In it 118 firefighters reported that they heard or witnessed explosions in the twin towers *prior* to their collapse (summary here[18]). Indeed, dozens of media sources reported here[19] that explosions were occurring before the buildings fell. A few hours after the tragedy those reports were never re-aired or investigated. Why? Are we to believe that all of those reports were in error? If that were the case why didn't any media source report this? Did the 118 firefighters all decide to retract their claims or have they instead been pleading us to listen? There is at least one organization of firefighters[20] that have been endeavoring to have their voice heard. They too are requesting a reinvestigation of 9/11. Are we to assume that this is instead an elaborate plot by "conspiracy theorists" to subvert the narrative for some hidden gain?

The accounts of the first-responders and firefighters that described witnessed explosions were mysteriously excluded from NIST's report. Was this an innocent oversight or a purposeful omission of testimony that would have redirected the entire investigation? It cannot be known with any certainty, but how are we to assess the media's role in this? Surely some investigative journalist should have explored this apparent lack of due diligence of an institution we have entrusted to not only explain why 2,749 innocent people lost their lives in the collapse of the twin towers but to ensure that our buildings are designed and constructed to standards that ensure public safety so that catastrophic structural failures will not happen again. Clearly the *absence* of such reporting has solidified the official narrative in our minds. Has this been their intent all along? What does your intuition tell you?

C. Why wasn't a "Controlled Demolition" Hypothesis ever considered?

Let us now take a closer look at NIST's decision to not search for evidence of explosive events during the collapse of the twin towers and Building 7. Their decision to not eliminate the possibility of explosives from the start not only defined the course of the whole investigation, it also represents a glaring example of a lack of scientific rigor. Why didn't they pursue this possibility especially in light of direct eye witness testimony from over a hundred firefighters that were part of the public record? Moreover, all three buildings in Manhattan fell in exactly the way buildings do when subject to explosive demolition. Did they have some *incentive to not look*? If so, what could it have been?

Let us say that they did decide to examine the debris for explosive material like other, independent teams did. What if they ended up finding some? Why couldn't they simply conclude that the terrorists rigged the building? What would be the problem in that? After all it wouldn't be the first time a terrorist organization attempted to blow up the World Trade Center with explosives. Everything would have still played out the same way, right? Not exactly. It would have led to the conclusion that security in the three buildings was so shoddy that this happened under their watch. It would have taken demolition experts months to set it up. It would be hard not to accuse the WTC security of being in cahoots with the terrorists. Suddenly things would start to point to a very real conspiracy.

If evidence of explosives were found the 9/11 Commission would also have to explain why planes were also flown into the buildings. That would be extremely difficult without abandoning the entire premise of the attack. This is why some immediately dismiss the possibility of a controlled demolition. If terrorists rigged the buildings with explosives, why would they sacrifice themselves by flying planes into them when they could have just pushed a button? Why even look for explosives if we all know planes hit the buildings? It is a compelling argument, but what *assumptions* are we making when using it?

When we dismiss the idea of controlled demolitions because we know that planes were flown into the buildings we are making a foundational assumption. *We are assuming that whoever orchestrated this wouldn't care if their identity would be revealed.* In other words, we are assuming that terrorists were responsible for this enormous tragedy. Terrorists wouldn't care if planes or bombs were involved. They would only want to be given full credit for the atrocity no matter how the buildings came down. Terrorists would demand that their identity be known, otherwise their effort would be meaningless to their cause, whatever that might be. It would be completely illogical for them to use planes and sacrifice themselves if they had already set up explosives in the buildings. *If evidence of explosives were found it would necessarily point to a conspiracy **because** planes were flown into the buildings too.* Hijacking planes on a given morning is one thing. Placing explosives up and down three Manhattan skyscrapers is a feat far more involved. The plane collisions *in lieu of evidence of explosives* would have been immediately identified for what they really were: **decoys** intended to distract us from the actual mechanism of destruction and more importantly, the identity of the real perpetrators.

Terrorists wouldn't need both explosives **and** planes, *only conspirators would.* As we watched in disbelief as two jet planes squarely struck those iconic structures on 9/11 and then watched in horror as they fell to the ground in seconds, few, if any would have suspected that a different mechanism could have been in place at the same time. However if the NIST investigation found evidence of explosives the implications would have been far reaching indeed. The significance of the plane collisions would dramatically change. Instead of being the obvious cause of the devastation they would become the undeniable proof of a conspiracy. Could this be the reason why NIST decided to not look for explosives even though there were so many firefighters and news reports confirming explosive events that morning?

If it were established that explosives were in fact used, attention would come to the sheer complexity of the effort required to bring three separate buildings straight down, synchronizing the charges so that the demolition would *appear* to be a gravitational collapse and not simply the detonation of explosives. This kind of endeavor would require more than 19 terrorists armed with box cutters. The magnitude of the possible conspiracy would begin to emerge. The forces behind such an act would clearly wield influence beyond what we consider possible in a free society. Entertaining such a thing is uncomfortable. It is no surprise that many wish to look no further. But do the governmental agencies that are entrusted with public safety have that luxury too? Perhaps they have been unwillingly doing someone else's bidding all along.

There is no proof of any of this as reported in any mainstream media source. It is a hypothesis that would explain all the impossibilities that exist. It would also give us a basis to dispense with the absurd and scientifically invalid collapse sequence NIST proposed while explaining the astonishing coincidences that occurred that morning.

D. How could this have been orchestrated?

Putting speculation about dark, hidden forces aside let us return to the practical aspects of how this could have been accomplished. The engineers that designed the twin towers insist that in order for the buildings to fall, the *central* columns had to have been compromised, not just the peripheral columns that the planes struck. Indeed, if you closely examine the initiation of collapse in the North Tower in this slow motion video here[21], it is apparent that the massive antenna at the roof is the first component to fall. The antenna is directly supported by the central columns. This is evidence that the central columns are failing first. There is no video that captured the extent of the damage inside the tower, but it is clear that the plane, which is essentially a hollow tube made of aluminum and fiberglass, had to first go through concrete and reinforced steel 14 inches thick. A plane's fuselage can severely damage concrete and steel columns if the energy of the collision was high enough. We all saw the gaping hole in the steel facade of both towers after the planes struck. It would be *impossible*, however, for the plane to remain intact after encountering the peripheral columns. Once again, this is Newton's third law of motion. If the steel on the outside of the building was destroyed, so too was the plane. To put it another way, the destruction of the peripheral columns is evidence that the plane must have been destroyed on impact. If you are skeptical that a jumbo jet would get destroyed by striking steel and concrete I would invite you to look at images of the extensive damage they sustain when striking birds. The laws of physics dictate that there would have been little left of the plane to damage the more sturdy central columns once they impacted and destroyed the exterior columns.

How could anyone have accessed the central columns of the twin towers for months, setting up the explosives? It seems preposterous that buildings of that size could have been rigged for demolition, even if there were enough conspirators involved. How could it have been secretly arranged in buildings that house tens of thousands of employees and visitors every day? Surely somebody must have seen something. How could this have been accomplished under the public's nose? It *seems* impossible. Then we have this interesting piece of information:

Twin tower elevator renovation[22]

This is a cover from Elevator World, a publication about elevator technology. In the spring of 2001 they reported that all of the elevators in both twin towers underwent a major renovation over a period of several months. The elevator renovation has been confirmed by people who were working in the twin towers before 9/11. The elevator shafts are surrounded by the central columns. This is obviously not proof that the elevator renovation in both buildings was a cover for the rigging of the central columns with explosives, it only offers a potential way this could have been accomplished without the public's knowledge. As unlikely as this may seem, the reality is that we are in the realm of *impossibility* when we try to explain the behavior of the buildings through a gravitational collapse alone.

The controlled demolition hypothesis explains the observed physical behavior of the buildings on that day. It does not identify perpetrators. It does not explain motives. Furthermore it does not answer the biggest question in our minds: If conspirators set up the demolition, *who were flying the planes?* Science will never be able to answer these very salient questions definitively. On the other hand, our governmental institutions did not even attempt to explain how basic laws of physics can be violated yet they were able to establish the identity of the perpetrators and what their motives were *before the third building even fell to the ground.* Nonetheless, it is their explanation that has continued to dominate our narrative for the last nineteen years.

Before moving on let us examine the troubling mystery behind the planes more closely. Clearly planes struck the twin towers. Does that necessarily mean someone was flying them? Whether you are aware of it or not planes can be flown remotely and far more precisely than even a trained pilot with thousands of hours of flight time. This technology has been in existence for sixty years. We the public now have access to previously classified documents surrounding a scheme proposed by military intelligence during the Kennedy administration to provoke the American public into supporting military action against Cuba by staging a fake attack on Americans and blaming Fidel Castro.

Here[23] we have the official memorandum from Kennedy's Joint Chiefs of staff outlining what was known as *Operation Northwoods*. On page 10 of the Annex to Appendix to Enclosure A the details of this proposed, diabolical plan gives us some insight into the minds of warmongers and the tools they had at their disposal as early as 1962. This document outlines the capability we possessed at the time to replace a civilian plane in flight with a remotely guided drone plane that was painted and outfitted to look identical to it. The drone could be flown and crashed into any chosen target while the civilian plane, now flying without a transponder signal, could be secretly landed elsewhere (e.g. to Eglin Air Force Base in Western Florida in this proposed mission). It would thus appear to everyone, from eyewitnesses to flight controllers that the civilian plane crashed (or in the Northwoods scenario, was shot down by Cuban fighter jets). It is difficult to overlook the eerie similarities between what was envisioned in the minds of the warmongering Joint Chiefs of Staff sixty years ago and the events of 9/11. Thankfully President Kennedy refused to condone such a plan.

This may seem like a desperate reach to argue for a conspiracy behind 9/11. However the official explanation violates basic laws of science that have served us for centuries. Objectivity requires us to consider all other explanations. There is yet another compelling reason to consider this possibility. An organized group[24] of professional pilots and aviation experts have been imploring the public to reconsider the idea that a person could have been able to pilot jet planes in the manner which we observed. They contend that it is impossible to fly these types of planes at just a thousand feet of altitude at the speeds that we all observed into such a narrow target. The twin towers were certainly very large but they were only about fifty feet wider than the wingspan of the planes that struck them. Runways that accommodate such planes are 25% wider than the twin towers but more importantly, planes are flying much slower during their approach to landing. The speed of the aircraft at the times of the impacts are even harder for these pilots to accept. The National Transportation Safety Board (NTSB) reported that the ground speed of the Boeing 767-200 that struck the south tower was 510 knots or 586mph. The *cruising* velocity of that model of plane flying at altitude where the air is much thinner is 541mph. Flying that fast with that level of accuracy at a mere 1000 feet of elevation where the air is much denser is a practical impossibility according to these experts.

To prove their case, some of these seasoned pilots who have thousands of hours of flight time flying similar jet planes to the ones that hit the twin towers attempted to duplicate the endeavors of the hijackers in flight simulators. They were never able to hit the buildings despite repeated attempts. The professional pilots could not match the miraculous flight skills of the hijackers. The idea that hijackers in cockpits of mult-engine jet planes for the first time in their lives flying this kind of sophisticated aircraft on a *suicide mission* knowing that the most advanced air power on the planet would be in pursuit could have struck their intended target not just once but twice is impossible for them to believe. The 9/11 Commission report states that their flight instructors described them as poor students. Several had difficulty completing their basic training and needed to re-enroll at other flight schools just to get a private pilot's license to fly single engine planes. Nevertheless we the public seem to have little problem in accepting that they were able to outperform professional jet pilots that morning. Clearly this is not due to our greater understanding of aviation and flight dynamics. It is due to *Source of Bias #2 (Unwillingness to look closer)* and *Source of Bias #4 (No capacity to understand the relevance of the information)*. The Pilots for 9/11 truth are not pointing fingers at anyone. They are asking our government to reexamine their explanation in the interest of truth. Who is to blame for our biases around this information and the fact that this group of professionals remain in obscurity?

E. How to manage the uncertainty around these events

Rather than reflexively labeling the controlled demolition theory as a crazy idea held by "9/11 Truthers" so that it can be conveniently packaged as a "Conspiracy Theory" and dismissed on moral and intellectual grounds, it is more apt to first focus on all the absurdities of the official explanation and not succumb to *Source of Bias #3: Unbalanced inquiry.* Hundreds of thousands of tons of steel breaking apart in seconds synchronously three separate times? A collapse sequence that violates the most basic laws of motion and energy conservation? Fires burning at Ground Zero for three months despite being submerged under millions of gallons of water? Four massive military exercises occurring on the very same morning as the attack leaving our Eastern seaboard largely undefended? A fourth plane "disintegrates" leaving little trace of human remains or luggage, yet a passport implicating one of the terrorists is found intact and legible at the crash site? Professional pilots telling us that it is impossible for them to duplicate the hijacker's flight skills? Over a hundred firefighters telling us that they were witness to explosive events prior to the "collapse" of the towers yet their testimony was not considered? Believing in the official story requires us to accept these events as either pure coincidence or unworthy of further exploration. Unless we are willing to accept the possibility that our accepted narrative is incorrect we have little chance of objectively exploring any counter argument (*Source of Bias #5: Overconfidence in an adopted opinion*).

Where are our other biases with regard to this transformative event? This is where the "Conspiracy Theory" label, if used indiscriminately and prematurely, can introduce bias. As we explored in Chapter 3, by labeling an explanation a "Conspiracy Theory" we are relegating it to the realm of unfounded. If there truly is no evidence of a conspiracy then this classification does not introduce bias. However, if the label is used *prematurely,* when evidence does arise it will not be examined objectively. It would be analogous to a judge telling the jury that a witness is a liar before his testimony is heard.

There is no question that suggestions of a conspiracy around 9/11 were prematurely designated "Conspiracy Theories". How can we make such an assertion? Very simply. The "official" explanation, with all of its impossibilities and inconsistencies was still not finalized until November 20, 2008, more than seven years after 9/11. Yet on November 10, 2001, seven years earlier, then president George W. Bush makes this[25] sobering statement as part of his address to the U.N. General Assembly just two months after that tragic day :

"We must speak the truth about terror. Let us never tolerate outrageous conspiracy theories concerning the attacks of September the 11th; malicious lies that attempt to shift the blame away from the terrorists, themselves, away from the guilty."

Two months after the disaster the President of the United States had already invoked the term "Conspiracy Theory" in front of the entire world. Beyond that he emphasized that any dissenting opinion regarding these events *should not be tolerated*. Not only is the judge telling the jury that the witness is a liar, he is instructing them not to listen to what he has to say.

President Bush was enjoying the greatest approval rating of his two terms. The country was shocked and mourning but unified behind our Commander in Chief. Why would it be necessary to characterize any and all alternative explanations as conspiracy theories, especially given the fact that very little of the physical evidence had been collected and analyzed? Fires were still inexplicably burning at Ground Zero under water when he made this statement. The "official" explanation with all its inconsistencies was still seven years away from release. There is no question that the use of the "Conspiracy Theory" label was made prematurely and arguably to great effect. You may jump to the conclusion that any argument regarding premature labeling is moot because we arrived at the "truth" eventually. Perhaps, but how could you be certain of that if we were biased to begin with?

A different set of perpetrators are not named in this "Conspiracy Theory". When we openly reexamine the events of 9/11 we end up pointing a finger at the media and no one else. It is their integrity which is under question. Have we held them accountable to acceptable standards of investigative journalism? More importantly, have they fulfilled their duty as our guard against tyranny as our founding fathers intended? I fully believe there are many, many diligent journalists whose integrity is not compromised, but there is a possibility that the few who control the organizations they work for have directed them away from the pursuit of the peculiarities surrounding these events, especially in light of the directive from the President of our Country. This is not so different a situation from the one we were in a century ago when JP Morgan had undeniable influence over our media channels and used it to his advantage.

This is where we must be particularly careful in our analysis. There is, of course, the possibility that our President was telling us to look away for a hidden reason. However, when we entertain this idea we are bringing in another "dragon" that can easily derail our pursuit of objectivity. The inescapable fact is that the public was told immediately after 9/11 that entertaining any other explanation was not to be tolerated *before anyone knew all the facts.*

We are again playing the role of a juror, this time deciding on the integrity of the media. This places us in a difficult but not an untenable situation. If we begin by asserting that our news organizations would not or could not misrepresent the facts of such a matter we are forced to accept the improbabilities and contradictions of the conventional narrative as extraordinarily coincidental. We would be falling into the trap of confirmation bias by establishing the truth of the matter first and then rejecting any evidence that overturns that truth. *In fact, this is exactly what the official report does.* Perhaps this is why we as the public have been so willing to accept our media's approach to this event. NIST begins and ends with the single hypothesis that two plane collisions and resulting fires and nothing else could have caused the destruction of *three* skyscrapers and dismisses or denies the existence of any evidence that refutes that hypothesis.

Nearly all elements of this story, from the identities of the perpetrators, their means, motives and ideologies had been established before the sun had set on Manhattan on 9/11. Having an explanation offered us a rope to cling to as we were thrown off a cliff of stark uncertainty that morning. Whether or not the "official" explanation was correct, accepting it outright, although comforting and perhaps excusable at the time, was not a decision made from objectivity.

To be objective we would need to examine all the components of the official narrative separately and estimate their plausibility independently of the others, just like we did in the hypothetical murder case in Chapter 2. What are the chances that the terrorists happened to pick the morning that most of our squadrons were conducting live exercises far away from the Eastern seaboard? What are the chances that on that day three buildings completely veered from predicted models of behavior and instead fell through their own supporting steel skeleton landing directly on their own footprint exactly like a controlled demolition killing nearly all the people within them including the first responders? What are the chances that for three months following 9/11 ground zero was the only place on Earth that steel girders could be submerged underwater and remain so blazingly hot for so long? What are the chances that NIST's admission that they could not find a way to get their computer simulation of building 7 to match the observed behavior of the building was an innocent oversight or irrelevant piece of information? What are the chances that a plane could crash into a cow pasture so violently that it left little trace of fuselage, luggage or human remains yet a hijacker's passport would survive intact and legible for us all to see? How likely is it that hijackers flying jet planes for the first time be able to exceed the skills of professional jet pilots twice in a row? Remember that each of these events were observed, uncontested and reported by the mainstream media themselves. In order to indemnify the media from a purposeful strategy to misrepresent or omit the facts *all* of these events would have to be viewed as plausible and unworthy of further investigation.

Imagine a headline in the New York Times or USA today that read : ***"Lawyers for Thousands of Professional Engineers and Architects challenge the 9/11 Commission findings in open court"***. At this moment the legal staff representing a professional organization called "Architects and Engineers for 9/11 Truth" is in fact petitioning the Southern District Attorney of NY State to convene a grand jury to hear and see the evidence that supports their contention that explosives were used on 9/11. These 3,200 experts (and counting) are members of their respective professional organizations. We rely upon them to design and build the structures that we all use. They are devoting their own time and money and, because of our societal biases, jeopardizing their personal reputations in order to bring public scrutiny to what they believe is a grossly negligent and unscientific investigation that impacts all of our safety. *Why is this not being covered?* We must admit that if this headline did run tomorrow it would be met with confusion if not incredulousness amongst the public. This is a clear sign that we are, or have become, biased against any challenge to the official narrative, no matter what the source. A grand jury has yet to rule on the evidence, but *why aren't we hearing about it?* How is the media treating the dissenting opinion? Is this what we would expect from a free press?

There are undoubtedly many organizations that are requesting official bodies to reconsider information at any given time. Few of these efforts can be deemed newsworthy. However here we are talking about a group that the mainstream media has labeled "conspiracy theorists". By our definition this group does not have any evidence to support their claims. Why then are they going so far as to request a grand jury to examine evidence if none supposedly exists? Moreover this is a group of professionals that we entrust to build sound structures and protect them from fires in the interest of our own safety. Are their efforts to bring light to issues that concern all of us really not a matter of public interest? How are we to interpret the fact that their effort to educate the public, pursue legal channels and petition our government for a serious investigation continues to remain in obscurity? Is the media biasing us?

It is impossible to establish beyond any reasonable doubt what truly transpired on 9/11. Neither are we seeking to prove that the buildings were blown up. Instead we are demonstrating that NIST is wrong. By doing so we are challenging the integrity of the source of our information regarding this event, a task very achievable and imperative if we are interested in eliminating our biases, our conceptual ruts and cognitive blind spots.

Notice that the same basic theme is arising in this and the two previous chapters. We have two models of reality from which to choose. Most of us are like the folks that lived in town in the first chapter. We are not experts in physics, metallurgy, architecture or flight dynamics. We are relying on the honesty and integrity of others to sort things out. Ed is played by the government, or more precisely, the 9/11 Commission, their report and the supporting technical documents provided by NIST. Jack is the media, reminding us how airtight Ed's research is, how he is a trusted member of the community and church. Enter Lenny, the independent voice of those who live by tracks telling us Ed's method and explanation is all wrong. Lenny is a member of our society too but the moment he starts making a fuss about "the trains" Jack starts calling him a welcher, or more specifically a "Conspiracy Theorist". We convene at the church to sort things out. However there is no "Pastor" here. The closest thing we have to a Pastor is actually Jack who has been telling us for years who we should believe and why.

Ed's story is that two planes were hijacked and flown into buildings causing their complete destruction within two hours. According to Ed, it was obvious that was the only mechanism of destruction. So obvious in fact, that it was unnecessary to even look for another explanation. Ed tells us that if we question him we ourselves would be in cahoots with the guilty and supporting "malicious lies".

Lenny then gets his time on the stand. However instead of a single, uneducated person who happens to live by the tracks Lenny is instead played by a series of experts that start popping up, one by one. We hear first from the architects and structural engineers that say Ed's story violates basic laws of motion. Moreover they point out the truth that Ed never did the math himself. Although he had a truly impressive organization of applied mathematicians, engineers and scientists at his disposal (NIST), he instead chose to let someone else do it for him, and the critical numbers they used don't match NIST's. We hear from the Firefighters who say they heard explosions prior to the buildings collapse. Jack heard them too but for some reason will no longer admit to that. We hear from chemists and demolition experts who say the buildings fell exactly like demolished buildings and that explosive residues were found at ground zero though Ed felt that a search for them was unnecessary. Then we hear from the pilots who tell us that the planes that took off from their respective places of origin were not designed to fly as fast as we observed. In fact, they say that expert pilots could not have flown them in the way we witnessed, let alone hijackers. Finally we remember that Ed was hatching a plan to pull off a similar stunt with remotely controlled planes sixty years ago with the intention of misleading us. We are reminded of how we were in the same position a century ago, more or less. Back then it was clear to leaders in the community that Jack was not shooting straight with the public at the time. Jack's biased, pro-war editorial helped to convince us to enter WWI.

There is no judge. That role is also played by Jack who gets to decide who is getting a voice in the matter. Most of us have been aware that there have been "conspiracy theories" regarding the events of 9/11. I would argue that few of us were aware of how many different experts in different fields are questioning the official story and how cogent their arguments are. Jack has been characterizing them as irresponsible, dangerous and easily seduced by alternative theories. He has also either directly thrown them into the same boat as "science deniers" who continue to believe the world is flat or, at the very least, insinuated this. The public generally pictures the "9/11 Truther" as a zealot with extreme views screaming for a new government or no government at all. Though these elements exist in our society and wave the 9/11 conspiracy flag, those at the forefront of this movement have been patiently asking for a day in court and petitioning the government for another investigation through the only channels available. Jack continues to characterize this solemn effort as frivolous when he acknowledges it at all.

The professional pilots, architects, engineers and firefighters who are requesting another investigation comprise only a minority opinion in their respective professions. However they represent a much larger percentage of people in their fields *who have actually looked at the official findings themselves*. Architects & Engineers for 9/11 Truth (AE9/11Truth[26]) have obtained over three thousand signatures from their community of professionals who agree that a reinvestigation of 9/11 is long overdue. They challenge "debunkers" to gather that number of professionals to come forward and *publicly* support the method and conclusions of NIST's investigation. Richard Gage, a professional architect with thirty years experience, a member of the American Institute for Architects and founder of AE9/11Truth, has developed a series of three webinars[27] to educate Architects and Structural

Engineers about NIST's approach and findings. He states that "9 out of 10 architects that view this material have changed their position on the official narrative and believe another investigation is in order." What are we to make of such a fact? Is the "music" finally being heard by those who can appreciate it?

One by one Jack calls other "experts" that he claims to know as much as Lenny if not more. Admittedly I have not given voice to these counter arguments. Seek them out if you wish. They generally appear whenever you search under the topic of "9/11 Conspiracies Debunked." Each of them attempts to refute the testimony of every individual "Lenny" whom Jack calls a conspiracy theorist. Hopefully you have learned from Chapter 2 that it is important to not sequentially dismiss each independent piece of testimony and evidence and move on. That approach works only if you can be absolutely certain of the validity of each one. Establishing certainty is not possible for us lay persons.

Where does it leave us? First we must admit that we are not experts ourselves and that places us at a huge disadvantage. How can we know the facts if the experts themselves seem to disagree? Jack is not an expert either, yet he is choosing who is the "real" expert and who is a "Conspiracy Theorist." By doing so he is deciding what the facts are. We are granting Jack a level of expertise that he claims we do not possess, the ability to be purely objective. Are we being too presumptive when we assume that Jack has the capacity to sort through matters of science--a subject he knows no better than we do? How does Jack make his determination about all of this if he is not a scientist himself? Clearly his methodology must be based on something outside of science and is therefore problematic since we are dealing with scientific matters.

We are at an impasse. Are we biased as the public? We most definitely are. It is difficult to accept the fact that Ed would lie about such a big thing and that Jack would let him get away with it. That would destroy the community and would prove that we don't live in a free society. This would be *Source of Bias #6 (Presumed legitimacy granted to a source because of personal feelings)* and *#1(Something to be lost by the outcome)*. We are not the experts (*Source of Bias #4: No capacity to understand the relevance of* *the information)*, and we haven't looked closely at all the details *(Source of Bias #2 and #3 : Unwillingness to look closer and Unbalanced inquiry)* which has likely led to *Source of Bias #5 (Overconfidence in an adopted opinion)*. We have been happy to go along with Ed, Jack and pretty much most of the public for 19 years now *(Source of Bias #9: Presumptive of legitimacy of the majority)*. Furthermore we can admit that it would have been hard to dissent given Ed's characterization of the minority as "Conspiracy Theorists" who are telling "malicious lies to shift blame away from **themselves**". Notice how Ed isn't just telling us that dissenters are mistaken and are thus making baseless arguments. *He is saying that they are lying and **are to blame**.* This of course invokes *Source of Bias #10: Repercussions of being the Minority*. Finally, the possibility that Jack and Ed could be working together to deceive us seems impossible. How could a conspiracy that big ever get pulled off without someone coming forward? In fact that has been a big part of Jack's argument all along. This is *Source of Bias #11 (Using the credibility of the conclusion to assign credibility to the evidence that supports it)*. I would argue that this is the most important source of bias to recognize here.

If you have managed to absorb the rather detailed scientific explanations in this chapter it is very likely that you sense that there may be something to it all, but ultimately it would require the cooperation of an enormous amount of people in different key positions in government and media. We may accept what our physics teacher tells us is possible and what isn't but unless you work with these concepts everyday it doesn't really sink in. In other words, we "believe" the science but we "know" that a conspiracy of this size could never be pulled off without someone coming forward. This is the power of knowing as opposed to believing. However knowing requires a perspective that is truly free of bias. Such a perspective is difficult to reach with regard to 9/11.

There are thousands of architects and hundreds of pilots and fire-fighters trying to tell us that we need another investigation. These people may be knowledgeable and earnest but in our minds they are not true whistleblowers. They are making their claims based on what they know, topics outside our basic knowledge. Our judgement about the whole thing often rests on the fact that nobody has come forward admitting they helped set up explosives or saw someone doing so. We are not being unreasonable by adopting this position. After all, we each view the world through our respective lenses. However it is important to ask yourself how likely it would be that someone who was involved in the surreptitious demolition of the buildings would decide to admit their role in such a heinous act. If a handful of people were witness to different parts of this potential conspiracy what proof would they have? Moreover, what proof would be necessary to shift our understanding of this event? A photograph or video of masked individuals in an elevator shaft? An elaborate document describing the entire plot with an official stamp on it? Or simply their oral testimony and their pledge to tell the truth? How much voice would they be given today? Would Jack give them a platform or would he instead categorically dismiss and vilify them as attention-seekers or part of a dangerous, anti-establishment, fringe movement seeking to destabilize this great country? Jack is playing the biggest role in this. Is he carrying out his duty to diligently communicate the truth without prejudice, hidden motives or influence? What do **you** feel?

At any given moment our ancient predecessors were aware of little more than what they could see with the naked eye. Today we hold a view of the entire world in our minds. That "view" is generated by an incredibly powerful and influential network of a handful of media organizations. These platforms now serve as our "eyes" onto the world. Are we truly seeing what is happening or is it time for an eye exam? History has proven that this institution, arguably the most important pillar of a free society, has not been invulnerable to influence from powerful players in banking and industry.

This is indeed a delicate matter and requires a certain presence of mind to look beyond knee-jerk reactions. Considering a different explanation of the events of 9/11 does not dishonor the brave first responders, the innocent people who lost their lives that day or the hundreds of thousands that have died and suffered in the nineteen years since. In fact it may shed light on the possibility of a profound truth about humanity. Instead of a world where no-fly-zones and walls separate good from evil perhaps we live on a much different planet. A planet where the vast majority of its inhabitants are actually peace-loving and cooperative but have been *taught* to be fearful and angry by the tiniest fraction of us who would benefit from such a climate of antimony and adversity. Is it possible that this has been the case all along? Perhaps we may have always been a peaceful species and not a belligerent one that can never escape perpetual conflict as we are often told. Unseen powers may very well be "playing on every prejudice and passion of the American people" just as they were accused of doing a century ago.

Was 9/11 actually a "glitch in the matrix" and not the proof of terror around the corner that we have been told? Did the true perpetrators inadvertently tip their hand, especially in regard to Building 7? As stated previously, few of us were made aware of its destruction on that day or in the days since. I would like to close this chapter with one more peculiarity surrounding the reporting of the destruction of building 7, also known as the Salomon Brothers Building. This[28] is a clip of the live coverage from the BBC that evening. BBC correspondent Jane Standley is reporting that Building 7 has just tragically fallen from damage it sustained from the twin towers' collapse earlier in the day. The problem is that Building 7 is visibly *still standing* in the background. Building 7 remained intact for a full twenty minutes after this report was aired. What can explain such a lapse in reporting accuracy? Yes, lower Manhattan was in ruins at the time but *no other building had fallen that afternoon.* There would be no way for someone to confuse one falling building for another. Are we to believe that a reporter could have (1) mistakenly identified a standing building as one that has collapsed, (2) report it to their correspondent in the BBC who airs it and then, (3) *by pure coincidence that same building unexpectedly happens to fall twenty minutes later?*

Neither Ms. Standley or any person at the BBC (or anyone on this planet) were witness to the destruction of the Salomon Brothers Building when her report was aired. It hadn't happened yet. Rather than reporting events as they themselves observed, it is more likely that here the BBC was simply relaying information to the public as reports were being released from the authorities on the ground. This is entirely reasonable however it begs the question, *why did the authorities get it wrong?* Is it possible that they had some foreknowledge of the building's impending destruction that was miscommunicated to the BBC?

Madhava K. Setty, MD

Foreknowledge of a building's collapse brings up very serious questions and contradicts NIST's position that the mechanism of building 7's collapse was unprecedented and could not have been foreseen. This is also part of the reason why they claim it took so long to explain. In any case, it is impossible to predict the exact time when any unstable structure will fall. Once a building is deemed unstable it is brought down in a controlled fashion, either with heavy mechanical equipment or if necessary, explosives. If the authorities believed that building 7 was threatening to fall and needed to be brought down it would have required explosives. It was far too large to raze any other way. This would have been a sophisticated endeavor requiring detailed planning and execution by a large team of demolition experts. Obviously this could not have been set up in an afternoon. What then are we to make of this clip moments before the collapse of WTC 7[29]? In this CNN report the police and firefighters are telling people to "keep your eyes on that building, it is coming down, *it is about to blow up.*" The scientists and engineers at NIST took seven years to formulate a nonsensical explanation that could not account for the symmetric and uniform manner of building 7's destruction, yet the police and firefighters seemed to have had a pretty good understanding of the situation and what they were told to do: clear the area so that nobody will get hurt from a building that is about to be demolished.

It is important to note that in my scrutiny of the BBC's coverage I am not insinuating that Jane Standley and her team are being purposefully deceptive. They aren't knowingly participating in a conspiracy. They are dutifully reporting on events as information was brought to their attention. When we suggest that the media is party to a few, very large conspiracies we are not indicting every individual journalist, reporter, correspondent or producer involved in creating content for the public. In fact very few, if any, need to participate or be complicit in a deception for it to transpire. The real issue is with the authorities who, from time to time, require the unwitting service of media outlets because they command our attention with their channels and our trust with their stamp of approval. How much of the narrative from that day was being pieced together by reporters on the ground and how much was being relayed from a central authority or information dispatch center? I posit that most of the details were authentically reported, including the dozens of reports of explosions being heard in the twin towers before they fell. Interestingly, **those** reports were never addressed again that day or on any other day since. This may well be more evidence that the greatest ally of the public can quietly become someone else's pawn when necessary.

In this effort to bring clarity to this event by offering a more plausible explanation one significant question remains unanswered. This is the question of motive. The controlled demolition hypothesis can explain everything that was observed. This is not true of the official explanation. However with regard to motive the official explanation clearly outshines the alternative one. The controlled demolition hypothesis cannot identify the perpetrators nor their motive. We have been told that the hijackers were motivated by their hatred of America and what it represents. At the surface this serves as sufficient explanation and enough for us to respond in the manner in which we have.

On the other hand, if this were the work of conspirators and not terrorists, it forces us to reexamine the impact of this event from a broader perspective. Why would anyone besides terrorists want to destroy three buildings in Manhattan and damage the Pentagon? Perhaps the motive of the *true* perpetrators was not to terrorize the population of a country that holds liberty and justice as its highest ideals but to *provoke* it into a predictable response to such an attack. Many, many people have suffered immensely from this event. Has anyone benefited? Could it be the same institutions that benefited from war a century ago? What is your intuition telling you?

CHAPTER 8:

What's that up in the sky??

*"When you call yourself an Indian or a Muslim or a Christian or a
European, or anything else, you are being violent. Do you see why it is
violent? Because you are separating yourself from the rest of mankind.
When you separate yourself by belief, by nationality, by tradition,
it breeds violence. So a man who is seeking to understand violence
does not belong to any country, to any religion, to any political party
or partial system; he is concerned with the total understanding
of mankind."*

—Jiddu Krishnamurti

In chapter 4 we examined what was arguably the biggest paradigm shift of our entire history as a species. Through the centuries-long and collective efforts of astronomers and mathematicians the Catholic Church's doctrine concerning our place in the heavens was irrevocably overturned--but only after about a millennium, give or take. A false narrative can persist in our collective consciousness for embarrassingly long periods even though it could have been, in retrospect, easily "debunked" at any time. Clearly much of the inertia around a shift in understanding is the result of the commandeering and distribution of information. From the 5th to the 17th century, that part (in European civilization) was played by the Church. These days, our media has taken over that role. Whether or not you regard the media as worthy of such a pivotal responsibility is ultimately a matter of your own opinion, however the fact remains that unless you live by the tracks you get your information through one form of media or another.

What other factors contribute to our sluggishness around clarifying our understanding of things? One factor is the *size of the misconception* that we are trying to liberate ourselves from. We may be quick to think that subtle misalignments in our understanding tend to persist because they may go easily unnoticed. History, however, has demonstrated at least once that the depth of the misconception is directly related to its longevity. For example, when reassessing the relationship between the Sun and the Earth, our minds were resistant to entertaining such a radically different paradigm. We may all be willing to accept that we could be off by a bit, but being VERY wrong is not just difficult to accept, it can be inconceivable.

Who decides what is "Newsworthy"?

In Galileo's time the Church exacted merciless control over the dissemination of information and ideas. Now in our time we are faced with the possibility that other forces are using the media to suppress truths about our banking industry (for example) and/or about transformative events like 9/11. If those who control the media are indeed engaged in a misinformation campaign, suppression is not the only tool at their disposal. Beyond the deliberate suppression of important truths or opinions they also have the power to influence how we stratify the importance of the information we are being fed. For example, by running a story on the front page with a large headline they are suggesting that the story is not only very significant but that the facts that support the story are unassailable. On the other hand, if a story appears in the rear of a publication with little fanfare, we can assume that what is offered has limited appeal, significance and may still be evolving or open to further investigation. We are indirectly being told where we should be placing our attention. This does not mean they are routinely disingenuous; I am only pointing out the reality that they have this power.

As recently as 2019 multiple mainstream media sources have reported events that should have rocked the globe. A story arguably more impactful than the Church's admission that the stars, planets and Sun are not in fact rising in the East and setting in the West but that the Earth is in fact *spinning*.

In May of 2019 the New York Times and CBS[30] reported that the US Navy has recently admitted that their pilots have been observing objects that defy our understanding of how things are supposed to fly. The incidents reported here occurred in 2014 and 2015. Another confirmed encounter referenced in the story involved a squadron from the USS Nimitz which occurred 10 years earlier. This is the "tic tac" sighting, where several pilots observed a small, elliptical "craft" moving in irregular paths at speeds exceeding what was thought possible. Recently, CNN again reports here[31] that the Navy has confirmed that their pilots have encountered UFOs. Is that such an earth-shattering admission? They are objects. They fly. They cannot be identified. So what? The real question is, if the Navy doesn't know what they are, *what are they*? We as the public are left to speculate and fantasize as we await the next morsel of information from our trusted government and news sources.

Why have they left us scratching our heads about this? Our military, through public channels, is letting everyone know that they are certain that something is out there. If they were entertaining the possibility that these new kinds of craft, capable of unthinkable speeds, maneuverability and access to a seemingly limitless amount of energy (they were noted to hover for hours at a time) were from a foreign country, would they have allowed the media to distribute their findings? No. It would have been a matter of utmost national security. If our government withheld their estimates of the strength of the steel in Building 7 in the interest of "national security", how should we expect them to treat the possibility that another country has technology that exceeds ours by a large margin? Clearly they have determined that these craft do not pose a threat to us, they are apparently of *unknown* origin and they move magically. Is an ET presence in our skies deserving of any more attention than it has received? Should this have been on the front page of every newspaper everywhere in the world? Attempting to answer this question requires us to examine the implications of this phenomenon more closely. In doing so we are also considering a more fundamental question: Who ultimately decides how "newsworthy" a story is?

Many people continue to regard these sightings as a curiosity, a preliminary chapter in a story that will end with the admission of a computer glitch, faulty radar system or errant weather balloon. Those who have followed the history of UFO sightings will undoubtedly conclude that this is the first crack in a wall of military secrecy surrounding *thousands* of separate Extraterrestrial spacecraft encounters that have occurred over more than seven decades.

The broad chasm between "believers" and "deniers" exists because the standards of proof on each side are not the same. On one extreme are those who require ExtraTerrestrial beings, *if they do exist,* to appear at town hall meetings before reconsidering their position. On the other are those who see a shaky video of amorphous lights appearing in the sky and then immediately conclude that E.T. is here. How then are we to assess the footage taken from the viewfinders of fighter pilots? We must acknowledge that if any more credence is given to this "evidence" it is only because of the credibility that we choose to bestow upon the source that has offered it. If we were to be purely objective, there isn't anything more here beyond the stamp of validity of trusted institutions like the US Navy and mainstream media. How then are we to proceed?

In this day and age, any form of recorded visual evidence (photographs and video) carries the possibility of misdirection. Even though billions of human beings have smart phones with sophisticated cameras at the ready, we must contend with the reality that photographs and video can easily be enhanced, modified or created from scratch to "prove" anything, including that an ExtraTerrestrial presence exists on our planet. If we cannot rely on video and photographs where then should we look for more reliable evidence?

Hypothetically speaking, unless one has had a first-hand personal encounter with a being from another star system, the most compelling evidence can only come from the testimony of actual eye-witnesses to UFOs. Could someone else's personal account offer anything more than an unsubstantiated, fantastical story? That is a matter of opinion. On the other hand, eye-witness testimony, though flawed at times, is often offered as the foundation of proof in our legal system today. If witnesses can condemn a suspect of a crime or provide an alibi that leads to their exoneration why wouldn't we consider testimony with regard to the UFO phenomenon just as seriously? The difference is that we cannot conceive of such a possibility to begin with. It would require us to abandon the deeply held understanding that we are alone because anyone else, if there is anyone else, is too far away. Being that wrong about something that big is not just hard to accept; *it is inconceivable.* This tendency to remain entrenched in a deeply held paradigm is a result of *Source of Bias #11 : Using the credibility of a conclusion to assign credibility of the evidence that supports it.*

Dr. Steven Greer is an Emergency Room Physician who has spent over two decades tirelessly compiling and spreading evidence of Extraterrestrial contact with humans and the possible suppression of this information by the media and governmental organizations. Two of his documentaries, "Unacknowledged" and "Sirius Disclosure" have been viewed by millions of people around the world. He has briefed members of Congress, former CIA Director James Woolsley and in 2001 held a conference at the National Press Club flanked by 20 retired military, FAA and intelligence officers who publicly attested to the presence of ETs on Earth. The conference can be viewed here.[32] In it these public officials are admitting that UFOs are absolutely real and have been internally acknowledged within the military for decades. If you take the time to watch this conference you may be struck by the electricity that was in the air and the tension that was in their voices. These officials seem to believe that they, whether by fate or grace, have been given the awesome honor and responsibility to finally let the world in on the biggest secret in its history. That was 19 years ago, and the public's attitude toward this topic has not budged. Is it because it is not newsworthy? Or are we being told that it isn't because it hasn't appeared in the news until now? Are these recent, isolated news reports commensurate with the significance of this story? To answer this question we must first get a handle on how old and how big this story really is.

Among the wealth of information he has made publicly available Dr. Greer offers over six hours of eyewitness testimony on his Disclosure[33] website, all of which is worthy of consideration. If you have ever listened to these interviews, it is difficult to conclude them to be intentionally misleading. The witnesses are mainly ex-military, some of them having held high positions. They have very similar stories with a few key, consistent elements including a typical military dead-pan delivery. Many were early in their military careers at the time of their encounter. They witnessed objects moving through the sky *soundlessly* at unthinkable speed, making maneuvers that would have crushed their pilots and then abruptly vanish. Their stories are often corroborated by other eyewitnesses and radar technicians. They claim that they were threatened by their superiors if they spoke out, so they waited, for decades in many cases. Now that their military careers are long over they find it meaningless to keep their promises of silence and wish to live out their remaining years with a clean conscience. There is, of course, the possibility that they are lying, but what would be their motive? They are not gaining fame or fortune for their candor. Most of them are unwilling to state that what they saw was from another planet or star system, they simply know that things just don't move like that, at least not anything from around here anyway.

How we choose to interpret these accounts, and more recently those of the F-18 pilots in the New York Times and on CNN, depends on your perspective and how flexible you are in your belief system. Here I would like to explore the "middle" ground. If you believe they are telling the truth *and* you also believe that ExtraTerrestrial craft are an absurd fantasy perpetuated by a pocket of our population that discounts Einstein's special theory of relativity (which dictates that "warp" speeds are impossible), it can only lead you to the following conclusion : the objects they saw are *real* and they are *from here*. In other words, secret military aircraft would explain most, if not all of the incredible stories told by people who seem utterly convinced of their experience and continue to remain undeterred in their account despite continuous attacks from "debunkers" and dismissal from every "real" media source. If you examine what we are being told from a scientific context this would be the most reasonable position to hold. However, it does lead to other questions...

The implications of Military Secrecy

The US military has been spending around $700,000,000,000 per year recently. Every once in a while we all get a glimpse of what some of this money is paying for when never before seen, radar-invisible, futuristic looking flying machines capable of classified speeds and unconfirmed altitudes that are made from obscure materials are rolled out of hangars with a modicum of fanfare. It is not unreasonable to assume that "we" have others out there being tested and tweaked. Flight testing is a necessary part of the development cycle of new technology and could explain many UFO sightings. It would also explain why the military has been so conspicuously tight-lipped about the whole thing until very recently. Why jump to the fantasy of ancient, interstellar civilizations that have found a way to crack the cosmic speed-limit when everything could be neatly explained by super-classified military flying machines running test flights?

The secret airship theory would tie up many of the loose-ends while not forcing us to discredit the earnest testimony of many eyewitnesses of unexplained aerial phenomena from our brothers and sisters in uniform. It does, however, introduce a new wrinkle in our understanding of the current state. If there are secret aircraft, *from whom are they being kept a secret?*

We may be quick to conclude that secrecy is a necessary part of modern warfare, and that having weapons technology up our sleeve endows us with a tactical advantage over our adversaries. Upon closer consideration, this military strategy has implications that are potentially very troubling.

To better explain, let us consider the advantage of secret weapons technology historically. In the closing months of WWII it became increasingly apparent that the empire of Japan had little intention of surrendering to the Allied Forces despite their continued heavy losses of life. Emperor Hirohito and propagandists worked the Japanese public into a frenzy through synergistic narratives of nationalism, honor and fear. The introduction of Kamikaze pilots, young warriors of sound mind that were willing to fly their propeller-driven planes directly into American ships gave the world a startling glimpse into the depth of Japan's resolve. The United States had something up their sleeve as well.

The possibility of harnessing the power of atomic fission through a chain reaction had been stirring in the minds of theoretical physicists long before the start of the war. The idea of turning this potential force of nature into a weapon came soon afterwards. The *Manhattan Project*, the secret effort of the US government to build the atomic bomb, did not take place in an isolated desert location in Los Alamos, NM alone. It was an enormous feat of science and engineering that required participation from not only theoretical physicists but engineers, mathematicians, material scientists, construction contractors and laborers. Thousands played a role and their efforts were distributed around the country, from New Mexico to Tennessee. To put it into perspective, the atomic bomb was not constructed entirely from stuff lying around the planet. Most of the Plutonium used in the Nagasaki bomb was *synthesized* from the bombardment of Uranium 238 with deuterium atoms. In other words, *another element* had to be brought into existence to accomplish this endeavor.

None of the public and only the tiniest of few of those involved with its production knew what the purpose of all of this activity really was about. Even the Vice President at the time, Harry Truman, was unaware that this effort was taking place. He took the oath of office on April 12, 1945 and was only then briefed about the extent and implications of the Manhattan project. Among other things, the success of our government had in maintaining secrecy around the Manhattan project serves to remind us that if coordinated correctly, *an awful lot of smart people can be kept in the dark about a lot of things, including their own role in a bigger plan.* This well-documented part of our history offers a potent counterargument to those who assert that a massive operation involving thousands of people, including some who hold high level positions in governmental institutions, could never be carried out without their knowledge.

The decision to deploy the first atomic weapon upon human beings was made behind closed doors. The successful test of an atomic weapon on July 16, 1945 (The Trinity Test[34]) demonstrated undeniably that our species had entered a nuclear age. By most historical accounts, neither the existence of an atomic bomb nor the results of the Trinity test were ever shared with the Japanese government prior to the bombing of Hiroshima three weeks later. Although it has been reported that a group of leading physicists involved in the development of the weapon formally requested that Truman reconsider his approach, they were not heeded. President Truman made the decision to drop the bomb with no specific warning to the Japanese about its potential for devastation. Ultimately he and his advisers believed that the impact of the bomb would be maximized if it occurred unannounced. Leaflets dropped on the people of Nagasaki referenced the weapon several days later. Because the empire of Japan refused to unconditionally surrender, that city was destroyed with another atomic bomb as well.

President Truman's reasoning has been subject to much scrutiny and debate. Regardless of one's critique of Truman, it is clear that the power of a weapon as a deterrent can only be utilized if the enemy is *aware that it exists*. One can argue that this has been proven as no nuclear weapon has ever been deployed on humans in the 75 years since the destruction of Nagasaki. Indeed, the hegemony nuclear powers exert over the rest of the world only exists because everybody knows who has them and who doesn't. What then is the intent of new kinds of weapons that are kept *secret*? Secret weapons cannot be deterrents against aggressive action. Weapons that remain hidden in secrecy are necessarily *offensive*. Moreover, secret weapons can serve a more diabolical purpose than the damage they inflict. If no one knows their damage signature, range or how they are deployed they can potentially be used to synthesize conflict and implicate innocent parties. How would anyone be certain of the source of the aggression? *Secret weapons do not exist to prevent wars, they exist to start them.*

Whether or not you consider a discussion around UFOs and Extraterrestrials to be flippant, the recent attention media has placed on this phenomenon offers an opportunity to consider the depth and implications of secrecy more soberly. Perhaps the US Navy has offered up this footage (15 years after the actual incident in the case of the "tic-tac" sighting) to be forthcoming. Regardless of their intent, it is important to put this admission into context. Are these the only sightings since 2004? Is it reasonable to assume that this recent disclosure reflects a spirit of transparency or have there been numerous other encounters with UFOs that official sources continue to refuse to acknowledge?

If these objects reported by the Navy are *not* of Extraterrestrial origin we must avail ourselves of the reality that weapons and craft of spectacular capability sit behind a wall of secrecy. Few of us take the time to consider what the implications of such a likely reality is. The last time the public was notified of a significant "advance" in military technology was the demonstration of the Hydrogen, or fusion bomb. The H-bomb is another type of weapon that harnesses the monumental energy of a nuclear chain reaction. These weapons are dozens of times more powerful than the atomic bombs dropped on Japan and whose yields are in the megaton range : the equivalent of *millions of tons of dynamite*. Yes, we can assume that these have become "miniaturized", deployable on a remotely guided missile or on strategic bombers that can potentially evade radar detection. Nonetheless, this technology is *70 years old*. To put this in perspective, the world had hydrogen bombs before we had transistor radios. Is it reasonable to think that the trillions of dollars that this country alone has spent on the military has gone merely to build submarines, smart bombs and incrementally faster planes? Or are there technologies hidden away that are unimaginable to a society that has been kept in the dark (for national security reasons) for seven decades. What does your intuition tell you?

Contemplating such things is obviously uncomfortable which may explain why we generally don't. Let us then return to the hypothesis that the "UFOs" the US Navy has encountered were indeed of Extraterrestrial origin. We are all aware of the subculture in this country that celebrates everything ET: from sightings to "landing sights" to "abductees". The public has grown to accept this element in our population like we accept a zany, harmless neighbor that lives a safe distance down the street: occasionally entertaining but never to be taken seriously.

How can we assess Proof of an ExtraTerrestrial presence on Earth?

Is there anything *real* behind all the UFO conventions and zealots in costumes? It depends on what you consider to be "real". As educated, discerning citizens we look to "established" journals and "official" sources to tell us what to believe. We must rely on our intuition to **know**. There are no articles in Scientific American or Astronomy Today that support the theory that there is and has been an ExtraTerrestrial presence on this planet. Sources such as these claim that there isn't any authenticated evidence of such a thing. Immediately we are faced with an inconsistency between trusted sources. Are these scientific journals discounting the authenticity of Navy pilots whose accounts corroborate each other? More importantly they opine that using a "little green men from Mars" theory to explain the unexplainable is wishful thinking or irresponsible hypothesizing. Better to leave things unexplained than consider a theory that would overturn deeply rooted and widely held beliefs. It seems a sensible position, but is it objective? It is not. This logic puts the cart before the horse: if there is proof that leads to an unreasonable conclusion, they say, the proof must be invalid or, paradoxically, inconclusive. Let us be very clear. Not all evidence of an ET presence on this planet is valid or conclusive, however if we qualify it as invalid or inconclusive *because* it leads to a conclusion that ETs must be here, we have allowed bias to enter our thought process *(Source of Bias #11: Using the credibility of a conclusion to assign credibility of the evidence that supports it).* If there were ETs popping in every once in a while how would we ever be able to prove it using this approach?

Despite what the public has been told by "established" scientific opinion and journalism there have been very diligent investigations that have uncovered very real evidence that requires the open-minded to ask some very serious questions. UFO sightings in this country alone number in the thousands per year. Of course many, if not most, can be attributed to "natural" phenomena. There are some that cannot. Over the past seventy years there have been thousands of encounters between people and "ETs" that involve testimony that can be corroborated by multiple sources, all standing up to lie-detector testing or confirmed through hypnotic regression. Hundreds have allegedly left evidence at "landing sites" that include ground markings or unexplained, residual electromagnetic perturbations at and near the sites.

As early as 1976 there were already over two-thousand such incidents that had been well-researched and documented. It is entirely possible that every such incident had been fabricated and the evidence falsified to perpetuate a hoax. If that is your belief, there is no point in examining this mystery any further. This is what our trusted scientific journals are proposing. However, if you are able to acknowledge there is a *possibility* that these events did in fact occur and can be considered evidence of an ET presence on here, we can get a better sense of where we stand.

Take the case of an incident that took place in the fall of 1973 in Pascagoula, Mississippi involving two men, Charles Hickson and Calvin Parker who claim they observed an oblong saucer descend near them while they were fishing on a river bank. Three creatures with grey skin, slit-like eyes and pincer hands approached them. Mr. Parker lost consciousness while Mr. Hickson, terrified and somehow paralyzed but conscious, was brought into the "ship" where he was "examined" by a scanning device for thirty to forty-five minutes and then left alone. He was eventually returned to the same location on the river bank. Both men were questioned extensively by the local authorities. They were then left in a room by themselves and secretly recorded. The eavesdropping authorities confirmed that the pair remained fearful and true to their story. Lie detector testing conducted by a "highly skeptical operator" confirmed that both men were telling the truth. Parker began to pray and eventually suffered a "nervous breakdown". Hickson suffered nightmares after the incident. He voluntarily subjected himself to hypnotic time regression. In these sessions he recounted his story as told while expressing authentic terror, which is difficult to "fake" under hypnosis. The investigation into this incident was conducted by Dr. J Allen Hyneck, Chairman of the Department of Astronomy at Northwestern University and Dr. James A. Harder, Chairman of Civil Engineering, University of California.

What are we to make of such a report? We may be ready to dismiss it because there is no *physical* evidence. But if there were physical evidence, how could we validate it? Even if there were, say, a piece of the "spaceship" that we could examine and hold, how would we ascertain that it wasn't just a piece of oddly patterned metal or plastic that we were handed? If there were reports from a metallurgy lab that confirmed that it was made of unknown elements, why would we trust the report? Is it possible to be objective? Again we come face to face with the reality that objectivity, in the absolute sense, is always beyond our grasp. We are forced, at some point, to trust another source. Even if we decide to only rely on our own direct experience we still cannot escape the possibility that our senses may betray us. One needs only to examine the plight of Mr. Parker and Mr. Hickson from their point of view to see this.

If we choose to dismiss the entire story because none of it can be absolutely verified we are not necessarily serving to best clarify our understanding of reality. Accepting the whole story as unassailable proof that ETs are here is also unhelpful. Notice that if you happen to dismiss the whole thing wholesale or accept it in its entirety you are doing so not from the validity of the evidence but more from your belief about ETs to begin with. You would be putting the cart in front of the horse.

In order to engage our intuition and/or pure objectivity we have to first drop our story about whether ETs exist or not and examine the story as it stands. There is the possibility the whole thing is a hoax conducted not just by a couple of guys with fishing poles but by the local authorities and the professors from Northwestern and the University of California. Keeping the possibility of intentional misdirection in consideration, if we examine the story at face value we can reasonably conclude that the two witnesses experienced something extraordinary and, as it turned out, debilitating. If we believe that the hypnotic regression, lie detector testing and bugged conversation between the two witnesses were conducted and reported faithfully there is a very high probability that the two men did in fact have what can best be described as a paranormal experience. However, attributing the experience to an ExtraTerrestrial life form is admittedly less certain.

What are the chances that these men did in fact have an encounter with ExtraTerrestrials? We cannot know. It is entirely subjective. The important point is to acknowledge that it may be highly unlikely *but not impossible*. We are placed in a similar situation as when we participated on a hypothetical jury in Chapter 2 when we sought to quantify the validity of the evidence of a murder or in Chapter 5 when examining reincarnation. Rather than being 80% certain of the "evidence" as in chapter 2, here we are probably a lot more skeptical. Rather than being 80% (or four-fifths) sure, we carry only a fraction of that kind certainty here.

The level of certainty you have about this story, offered as evidence of ETs, is entirely up to you. Just as in our hypothetical murder trial, there is more than one piece of evidence. There are now thousands of similar incidents, independently investigated and cataloged, all having more or less the same elements. If our trusted scientific journals are correct in asserting that ETs are no more than a fantasy in the minds of the gullible, then *every single one* of these events must have been staged or explained by some other, non-ET phenomenon.

From our inquiry into reincarnation we know that multiple pieces of evidence that can each independently overturn a paradigm will have significant influence on uncertainty. For the purposes of discussion, let us estimate that there is a *one in a thousand* chance that this encounter is authentic and inescapably proves that we are being visited by beings from another solar system. In other words we estimate that there is 99.9% probability that the mainstream media and established scientific journals are correct in dismissing this particular story as moot or inadmissible as proof of ET visitation. If we assume that the other 2000 or so such incidents all have more or less a one in a thousand chance of being authentic, what are the chances that they are all faked or inconclusive? Just as in the situation where you sat on a hypothetical jury assessing the validity of evidence we are now again determining the probability that our assertion that the "ET phenomenon" is a hoax. In other words, in order for the whole thing to be a hoax *every one* of the two thousand incidents must have been caused by something other than an ET encounter.

Probability that ETs do **not** exist = $(0.999)^{2000} = 0.135$

If we are willing to accept that each of these two thousand incidents carry just a one in a thousand chance of being an authentic ET sighting that means that there is an 86.5% probability that ETs *have been here* at least once. How does this number sit with you? Perhaps you feel that we have overestimated the validity of each of these events. Just like in Chapter 5 nobody is saying what number to plug into the equation--there is no "right" answer, we are merely exploring how much power multiple, independent pieces of evidence can exert upon a resulting conclusion. Note that if you wish to reassess your estimate of each piece of evidence *because of the result of our calculation*, you too are putting the cart before the horse.

We must admit that it is not easy or even possible to separate our assessment of the evidence from our feelings about resulting conclusions that would be earth-shattering. This is why paradigm shifts are so rare.

This is why it takes more than one photo of a dragon to prove they exist. But how many will it take? Two? A thousand?

As mentioned earlier, there were about 2000 such independent ET encounters that were inexplicable and supported by reasonable evidence as of 1976. The world at that time had been treating UFO sightings with at least, if not more skepticism than we do today. This is because for nearly 40 years after the "Roswell incident", where a flying saucer allegedly crashed into a rancher's sheep pasture in 1947, the US military had been flatly denying any possible connection between UFO sightings and ETs while insinuating that anyone who thought otherwise must be a few cards short of a full deck. How do you think these incidents would have been regarded by the public at that time if instead the US Navy had admitted through mainstream media sources that they too had been seeing and cataloging encounters their pilots were having with UFOs? Clearly there would have been more investigation and open discussion about the phenomenon. Yet this is where we find ourselves today. Is this really a story worthy of big headlines or has it been covered in a manner commensurate with its importance?

The significance of UFOs

To answer this question we have to look a little closer at the implications of the possibility that ETs might have been wandering through here from time to time. Of course, most of us are too busy to take any of this seriously. They're here. So what? What is the big deal? The fascinating part of this phenomenon, *if* it is real, is not about questions regarding who ETs are, where they are from or even why they are here to begin with. Our central question should be : "If they are here, *how did they get here*?".

In the mid 1970s NASA launched a series of unmanned spacecraft on missions to explore the outer solar system. Voyager 1 left our planet's surface in 1977 and continues to distance itself from the Earth at about 11 miles per second. It is one of the fastest moving objects we have built. Traveling at that speed would allow it to reach our nearest stellar neighbor, Proxima Centauri in about 70 *thousand* years, if it were headed in that direction. If there were ETs on this planet, presumably from neighboring star systems, they clearly have found a way to traverse space much more quickly than we can today. If it were possible to propel a spacecraft at speeds that would allow visitation of nearby solar systems within a decade or two, it means their ships would be approaching ¼ or ½ the speed of light, about 8,000 times faster than Voyager 1. Not only would fast ships be needed, it would require a way to avoid a collision with any kind of interstellar debris. Running into a pebble at ½ the speed of light would be the end of your trip. It is more likely that they would have found a different way of getting around.

Whatever means they may have would require a massive amount of energy. Where would such energy come from? Lithium batteries? Nuclear reactors? Solar panels? It is far more likely that it is from a source that we have not yet conceived of, one that would be limitless, safe and compact. It would also be from a source that is accessible from any point in the universe, including right here. In other words, a source that would be exceedingly useful to a species like ours that extracts fossil fuels out of our planet's crust and burns them in power plants and internal combustion engines. Is it true that *everyone* would benefit from such a technology? Is there anyone who would gravely suffer from the widespread use of such energy systems if they did exist? If this line of questioning seems vaguely conspiratorial, it is. However the inexplicable lassitude our media has demonstrated in pursuing such potentially monumental stories that are unfolding around us today forces us to reckon with such possibilities.

It certainly would be nice if a star-going civilization from Vega or Arcturus would stop by and loan us their "power packs" so that we could see how they work. Maybe they could even help us build a few million of our own to produce enough free, clean energy to power 10 thousand large cities. Perhaps that will happen someday, who knows? On the other hand, if they did make such an offer, would we, the citizens of planet Earth ever find out about it? Or would our authorities keep the technology hidden from us and let us continue on in the only way we know how? After all, free and limitless energy on this planet would change everything. Many industries are based on fossil fuel and internal combustion engines and the distribution of power to cities and homes. There would certainly be a few very powerful folks in this world that would be dismayed at this prospect. This is not speculation, this is how we react in a competitive environment.

How did wagon makers view the automobile? How do weapons manufacturers view world peace? How would a trillion dollar fossil fuel industry view free energy? Hypothetically speaking, if ETs with advanced energy systems have already offered this technology to our authorities how would we ever know or suspect it?

Bob Lazar and the Suppression of Technology

We must concede that if it has happened there would have to be yet another conspiracy afoot. The hypothesis that ET craft have crashed or have been shot down over the years is not new. It is said that their ships were taken to secret hangers and dismantled. The technology in them was then "reverse engineered"--a technical term for starting with the finished product and then dissecting it to see how it works. It is impossible to prove beyond a doubt that this has in fact happened. There has been some fascinating testimony from individuals who claim to have in fact done such work in such secret places. One such person worthy of mention is Bob Lazar, an engineer who claims he was recruited by the defense industry in the late '80s to figure out how the propulsion system for one of several alien spacecraft in our country's possession functioned. Mr. Lazar "outed" the facility and the kind of work taking place there 31 years ago on a local TV station in Las Vegas Nevada, and after a few subsequent interviews has lived in relative obscurity, shunning public attention until recently. The 2018 documentary "Bob Lazar: Area 51 & Flying Saucers" was co-produced by George Knapp, the investigative reporter that first aired his story three decades ago. Mr. Lazar has very little to substantiate his claims other than a sharp level of detail in his account, an unassuming attitude and a reluctance to bring attention to himself. None of these things would carry much weight in a court of inquiry. Indeed, if we use Wikipedia as our gauge of credibility, it labels him a "conspiracy theorist" in the first sentence of the entry.

On the other hand, like most ideas presented here, there is no way to irrefutably prove anything, including the possibility that he has been lying this whole time. The Lazar story is an example of a piece of evidence that would suggest that there has been an on-going effort to suppress a very big story about an ET presence on this planet. Again, the validity of the evidence is entirely subjective. No one is suggesting how much weight to give it. The important point is to either acknowledge that there is a possibility that his story is authentic or understand the basis behind your reason to reject it wholesale.

Before coming to any conclusion it is worthwhile to hear a bit of his story from his own mouth. Here[35] is a clip of Lazar answering some pointed questions from interviewer Joe Rogan. As you listen to his "story" notice if your opinion about his credibility is shifting. If it is shifting, is it happening from a place of objectivity or are you engaging a different aspect of discernment? Notice that at times he struggles to find words and cannot maintain his train of thought. How are you interpreting that? Is he attempting to fill in details of a story that he has fabricated or is he struggling to accurately convey a sequence of events that actually happened to him thirty years ago? Your opinion about this is important because it will either add to or subtract from the credibility you choose to grant him. This will directly determine how you view the rest of the story. Is he a conspiracy theorist? Or is he a whistleblower that has yet to be acknowledged by mainstream media? Using objectivity alone you will not be able to obtain certainty. The question is, how do you *feel* about what he is saying? If you think his story is preposterous do you *feel* that he is also being intentionally misleading? Those are two separate things. By "feel", I explicitly mean something other than *think*.

Before moving on let's take a moment to meticulously dissect Lazar's story and its implications. As we do we are also peeling the layers of our minds to hopefully gain some understanding about how we end up where we do. If you regard his story as pure fabrication, it is likely due to the sheer implausibility of his story. He didn't just claim to see lights in the sky or grey creatures hanging around a fishing hole. He says that he was given permission by *our military* to climb into a craft built by a civilization from another star system to attempt to figure out how it flew. "Flew" is a term that can only be applied loosely. The craft, he claims, came from a different star system and didn't even have a lavatory for its occupants. It didn't fly at all. It would be better described as a contraption that could move through space nearly instantaneously. Not only was it not of this Earth, it was more likely not entirely of this *dimension*.

If that weren't enough, he claims this craft was kept in a large hangar with a half dozen other ET "flying saucers" of very different configurations, perhaps from different civilizations altogether. He has absolutely no proof to back his claims. Why (on Earth) should we believe him? On the other hand, what sort of proof would suffice in this situation? A photograph? A video of him climbing into a flying saucer, zooming across the desert and landing it again? How would we authenticate it? If someone told us the video was authentic why would we believe them? What if someone else in the program came forward and vouched for him and his story? That doesn't make them whistleblowers. They could be *conspirators*.

Suppose an established, professional media source validated his story in its entirety. Why would we believe it? How would they have established the veracity of his story if they were forced to deal with the same questions we have raised here? The only real way we could be convinced that Lazar is telling the truth is if our authorities admitted their role in all of this. Until then they are innocent until proven guilty; a very reasonable attitude given the principles of justice we accept and uphold. However because the only proof we will accept of their guilt is their own admission of it, we are not being objective; we are being dogmatic. Bob Lazar can only be vindicated by the very party he is indirectly accusing of a massive set of lies.

The point of this exercise is to demonstrate that in our diligence to remain absolutely objective, free from distortion and only rely upon evidence that is irrefutable we end up in a paradigm that cannot be overturned while we remain in it. The trust we place in our authorities (or the media source of our choosing) is the axis upon which this paradigm revolves. Ultimately trust is not something bestowed from objectivity. It is a product of faith or intuition. How you *feel* about Lazar's account is more important than you might think.

An interesting aspect to Lazar's story is that he was not an abductee or a witness to inexplicable lights in the sky on some night. He claims to have been working on the most intriguing aspect of an ET "spaceship": its propulsion system and its means for generating power. He admits that only a modicum of progress had been made in understanding the technology by the time he was fired for going public. In the few interviews he has given he admits to having regrets about attempting to bring attention to this secret work, not because of the backlash he has suffered but because he has forever lost the opportunity to put his hands on what was likely the most spectacular technology to have ever existed on this planet. Lazar admits to being, above all else, a technophile and a geek.

Lazar's story is salient not just because it is potentially a source of uncertainty surrounding ETs on this planet but because it may point to the possibility of a more active and widespread suppression of advanced technologies by our authorities. The United States Patent and Trademark Office (USPTO) controls the dissemination of new ideas. The Invention Secrecy Act of 1951[36] formally gave this arm of the government the power to prevent the distribution of any new idea or technology that would pose a threat to National Security. This element of control is prudent. We wouldn't want the blueprints for advanced weaponry available to any person or institution that was willing to pay the inventor a royalty for using their idea. But how does the USPTO determine what kinds of ideas pose a threat to our safety? The real decision makers are the military (Army, Navy, Airforce), the National Security Agency, NASA and sometimes the Department of Justice. These agencies and institutions submit a list of categories of sensitive technology to the USPTO in the form of a Patent Security Category Review List (PSCRL). Technologies falling within these categories are subject to a possible secrecy order which bars the award of the patent, orders that the invention be kept secret and prevents filing of the patent with foreign agencies. Without patent protection the inventor has little to gain for making their idea available to everyone.

The specific patents that are under secrecy order at any given time are classified. However, in response to a series of requests for disclosure under the Freedom of Information Act made by the Federation of American Scientists we know that as of 2017 nearly six thousand separate patents are under a secrecy order. The specific application of these technologies remain classified. However we did get a glimpse of the *categories* our patent office deems worthy of a secret order when a previously classified list of categories (a PSCRL) from 1971 was made public. You can view the list here.[37] There are 23 general categories of technologies listed ranging from navigation systems to cryptography. We can feel confident when items such as Explosives (Group I), Missiles (Group II), Weapons and Counter Weapons (Group IV) appear here. Others seem rather arbitrary like Compasses (Group VIII, item 9), Underwater propulsion units for swimmers (Group X, item 15) or Low-level nuclear radiation detection equipment for detection from concealed sources (Group VI, item 8). These seem to have little bearing on national security and may even offer some benefit to us.

What is most troubling are items such as Solar Voltaic Generators *with efficiency greater than 20%* and Energy conversion systems with *efficiency greater than 70-80%* and Biochemical Fuel Cells (Group XI, items 8,9 and 6). Finally there is Group XXIII, Item 8: *Any invention directed to fuel economy, efficiency, air and noise pollution.* What would be the purpose of preventing the exchange and development of these kinds of ideas in the public domain on a planet that is desperate for new, efficient and clean sources of energy? If our government feels that Solar Powered generators that are greater than 20% efficiency should be kept secret how would they treat a compact energy source that is potentially capable of limitless output like Mr. Lazar was allegedly working on? Is this the real motive behind the suppression of an ExtraTerrestrial presence on Earth? These are vital questions to keep in mind as we consider the ET story. Whether Bob Lazar is telling the truth or not we can not use the apparent absence of such systems on our planet as proof that they do not exist behind closed hangar doors. Are we being kept in another Dark Age right now? How long would the last one have endured if the great minds of that time remained quiet, muzzled or worse yet, *ignored*?

Other "Hawks" in our skies

Let us say for the moment that such advanced civilizations do exist and have been here many times before. If they are capable of interstellar voyages they would have found a way to harness an incredible source of energy. Putting that energy towards the propulsion of a spacecraft or possibly even "bending" space is likely just one way to use the technology. No doubt there would be other uses, some very destructive. We can only imagine what kind of weapons could be built with such systems. We can infer that if there were civilizations from other star systems that found a way to make it here they would have little trouble subjecting us to their whims.

More reassuringly we can also assume that they would have long ago abandoned such things as wars. Why? If a species figured out how to explore the stars, it is likely that they would have long ago abandoned the idea of countries, borders and nationalities. Does it seem plausible that an ET from a planet 20 light years away would have launched her flying saucer from a "country" that was surrounded by walls and defense systems designed to protect it from another country with similar capabilities? Would there be things like racism or starvation on such a world?

You see, going interstellar is not just a small step from sending a probe to Mars. When we look up at our night sky planets and stars appear remarkably similar, but they aren't. The nearest stars are a *hundred thousand times farther away*. Using our most advanced spacecraft to get to the nearest star would be like using a bicycle to ride to the moon. Going interstellar represents a "quantum leap" in understanding and capability that would, more importantly, require cooperation on a planetary scale. This does not necessarily mean that every individual on a planet must make a large personal sacrifice to this endeavor. Rather it requires everybody to play nicely in the sandbox. It's hard to build a castle if somebody is constantly kicking sand in your face. We can postulate that such civilizations have made contact with dozens of other others. Perhaps they engage in missions of conquest but how likely would it be that they were struggling with *internal* conflict?

What sort of philosophy would guide a civilization of such capability? Would a concept of a "chosen people" or a "savior" that must be accepted at any cost exist in their psyche? It is doubtful. Those kinds of belief systems divide a population, not unify it. We don't have to look far to confirm this. If you disagree with this sentiment, take a moment to imagine how they might regard *our* saviors and chosen peoples. Hopefully it would be with tolerance and compassion and perhaps a tiny bit of amusement. At the very least we shouldn't expect them to accept ours anymore than we should accept theirs, if they believed in such things. If this line of reasoning is uncomfortable for you, notice if you have a resistance to accepting the possibility of Extraterrestrial existence on our planet *because* of this discomfort.

In our world, the endless wars that have resulted from differences in religious doctrine have really been just a struggle for supremacy on a very limited stage. We have been fighting each other in a tiny sandbox not knowing that it sat in an enormous playground. A species with interstellar capabilities would likely have encountered hundreds of planets, thousands of cultures and trillions of individuals. The concept of "supremacy" would be laughable when playing in a sandbox that is literally *infinite*. Perhaps there would arise the desire to be the biggest kid on the corner of the galaxy, but the inhumane suffering and loss of life on Earth have often been the result of wars fought on absolute terms. A star-going species would have long ago dispensed with aspirations of "total" domination. How could such a thing be achieved on limitless scales? Total domination is a possibility that only exists in limited perspectives held by limited minds.

It invites us to consider the possibility that we have been assessing our progress in a misleading way. Rather than considering the sum of what we know and can do as a representation of our progress perhaps we should instead be gauging our achievement by how much we are able to acknowledge what we *do not know and cannot do*. In other words, when we compare civilizations it may be more apt to weigh how each estimates what lies outside their own capabilities than within them. The more you know, the more you know what you don't know. Perhaps humility is the best measuring stick to use when sizing up truly advanced civilizations.

The existence of ExtraTerrestrial beings on the Earth, if proven and accepted by all would be more than just a curiosity. It would be the beginning of a global awakening. Why? Because sooner or later we would ask ourselves, "If they could achieve such things, why can't we?" At that point we would be forced to take a hard look at ourselves in the mirror. It is obvious that we have been regarding our progress as a species from a purely technological perspective. That may only be a small part of the picture. If there *were* a recipe for the evolution of a species like our own perhaps the "ingredients" may not be as important as the "process". In other words, maybe it is essential that we learn to cooperate *before* we start advancing technologically. The kind of technologies that arise from a belligerent mind will be different than a cooperative one. If that isn't immediately obvious, why then did we end up with an atomic bomb before a nuclear power plant? Could this be the reason why our neighbors from Vega (if they did exist) are "ghosting" us and not sharing more? There would be no reason for an advanced civilization to share technology that could be weaponized with a species that has been perpetually locked in conflict. Their apparent absence may be the best indication of their benevolence.

If we do not learn to truly cooperate on a global scale we may forever remain yoked to a trajectory that will never allow us to rise to our full potential. That potential would be on full display every time a contrivance from *another star system* moved across our sky. Whether we wanted it or not, it would be a dose of humility that we desperately need to really move forward.

Nature has been an excellent teacher. By keenly observing the examples she has provided we now can see far better than hawks. Nature did not give us the blueprints for the Hubble telescope, instead by offering us the hawk she gave us an inkling of what is *possible*. ExtraTerrestrials, if they existed on Earth, would demonstrate that we have been living with a different kind of blindspot. This is not one that has hampered our vision of the external world; it is one that has limited our capacity to self-examine. Do other "hawks" fly in our skies? Are they being kept from our view not because they pose a threat to us but because our knowledge of them would threaten those that keep them hidden?

Nearly everyone, at one time or another, has wistfully imagined a world with no war or hunger, but why have we not been able to *actualize* it? Is it because deep down in our collective psyche we don't believe it is possible? What would happen if an ExtraTerrestrial presence on this planet was acknowledged by all? How much war would we be willing to stomach if we knew there were civilizations more capable and more intelligent than us quietly sitting on the sidelines watching us bludgeon each other over spoils that they considered worthless? We have grown to accept the idea that life is a struggle and that we must protect ourselves from *each other*.

Is this our inescapable nature as homo sapiens or have we been *nurtured* into upholding this paradigm?

ExtraTerrestrials and our True Nature

Putting the Earth at the center of creation was a paradigm that could not be overturned through observational astronomy alone. In order to dismiss it we had to first accept a new and initially unrelated theory, that the motions of large objects could be *predicted* based on their mass. When that model was proven, accepted and held in combination with what we observed from the ground a different but more accurate model of our solar system could be accepted. The proof we searched for in our telescopes could never be found. The proof came out of left field.

In chapter 5 we examined the futility of looking for a source of consciousness in our physical body, yet we remain reluctant to move beyond this paradigm until we have sufficient proof. Dr. Ian Stevenson, widely considered to be the world's expert on reincarnation, admits that without a defined *mechanism* of soul progression nothing can be proven. But how could we ever find a mechanism of such a thing if we look no further than the molecules that make up our bodies? We seem to be just as stuck as the star-gazers were four hundred years ago. If there were a breakthrough, from where would it come?

What would happen if we regularly observed an example of a society that has chosen to fully cooperate on every level, not just for a day or a decade but for a few million years? As usual, we can only speculate, but we can predict that if ETs were around we would eventually ask ourselves (or them directly) how they managed to do it. What do you think the answer would be? Did they stumble upon a chemical that reworked their DNA (or whatever molecule encoded their cellular blueprint) so that they self-evolved into a cooperative species? Do they have a central authority that forces them to be placable? Did they just wake up one morning and decide to treat each other "humanely"?

I suggest that if they do exist, they were once like us, psychologically tied to a limited physical existence. They may have suffered similar consequences of separating themselves into groups with different ideologies and "identities" that eventually came into conflict. As long as they upheld the idea that they were individuals that would cease to exist after their bodies perished, the deaths that resulted from their wars were seen in absolute terms, rarely forgivable and often justifiably avenged. Conflict would get perpetuated. The idea of permanent peace and cooperation would have been a pipe dream to them until one day one of two things happened. They began to listen to their children who had been remembering their past lives. When taken to heart (or their corresponding organ of circulation) they would have seen that death was not what they thought it was; it could be forgiven for it would result in another birth. More importantly it would lead to an experience that any species that *knows* it reincarnates will eventually have: everybody will see themselves in everybody else. Whether you remembered it or not, logic would dictate that at one time or another you played the role your adversary or tormentor is playing right now. The group of souls incarnated at any moment are more or less the same ones that not only created their own history but are creating their own future. The only logical course of action would be to forgive and fully cooperate. Either that or continue to suffer at the hands of each other interminably.

The other possibility is that they were, in their remote past, visited by a more advanced civilization and found themselves in precisely the same position we may be in now, asking how *they* managed to get it together. The significance of ETs on our planet may be more deeply tied to our understanding of ourselves and our fate than we think. If this seems a preposterous theory out of left field, it is. I would argue that it is less preposterous than using telescopes or microscopes to search for proof in places where it cannot be found while believing that this approach is somehow rooted in logic.

The point here is that it is very unlikely that a planet of "intelligent" beings would find a way to cooperate with each other for more than a few generations if they believed that their death was the end. Truly moving forward would require more than just an upgrade in their technology. It would require a deeper understanding of themselves. This is, for the moment, nothing more than an intriguing hypothesis that may or may not be applicable to our species. It seems clear that we are waiting for something more concrete before we would ever consider such ideas actionable. What are we waiting for? Once again, I suggest that it is one of two things. The first is that we collectively run the experiment on a global scale and see what happens. If we decided tomorrow to drop our weapons and cooperate for a few hundred generations and dutifully record the results as any good scientist would we may see that this is indeed the right way to go. Obviously this is not going to happen.

The other is that we wait for an example of a civilization that has run the experiment themselves and openly assess *their* results. Is it possible that this is in fact what is happening right now?

There could be a profound elegance and purpose behind the scale of our universe, at least what we understand of it. Traversing the void of interstellar space, if it were possible, seems like it would require an unerring dedication to cooperation on a large scale. Without the staggering distance between stars we could predict that belligerent, marauding species with rocket powered ships could find their way to other, less advanced civilizations on nearby worlds, one after the other. The results would not be hard to predict. After all, we all live on a planet that represents this model on a smaller scale. Rather than viewing the universe as mostly cold and empty, it is perhaps better seen as an environment particularly well suited, with its built-in buffers of immense oceans of interstellar space, to allow intelligent civilizations to evolve to a certain level of understanding before it can influence others. The scale of the universe would naturally select for more compassionate interactions between truly advanced civilizations, if there were any.

What to make of all this? Perhaps you consider the ideas presented here fanciful. It's up to you to decide. The reality is that there seems to be some very convincing evidence of something very big going on up there. Is it getting the attention it deserves? Who is ultimately deciding what is worthy of our attention?

CHAPTER 9:

It's all in your head

Today in middle school classrooms around the world our children are taught that everything we can see and touch are made from tiny particles called atoms. The atoms are so small that they cannot be seen with our eyes or even a conventional microscope. Atoms are tiny compared to the wavelength of light, the means by which we see things. If something is so small that it cannot deflect visible light, it will forever remain invisible to eyes like ours. We know they exist because of the keen observations of scientists who first noticed the seemingly random, tiny motions of dust on alcohol or pollen grains in water under a microscope. Years later a rather innovative thinker by the name of Albert Einstein postulated that these motions might be the result of collisions with millions of very tiny particles of water called "molecules" and derived equations that would explain such motions if molecules did exist. Further observations seemed to hint that these molecules and atoms had an internal structure built from components that carried an electrical charge. Visionaries, mathematicians and researchers stood on the shoulders of their predecessors to give us a peek into the realm of the very small. Using electron microscopes that direct beams of electrons at a target we have been able to take pictures of individual atoms.

The question is, when did we prove that atoms actually existed? Was it when Einstein offered a way to describe the observed micromovements of tiny particles through a mathematical formula? Was it when another scientist, also of legendary stature named Ernest Rutherford irradiated a thin foil with a high powered stream of particles and demonstrated that most of them passed through the foil but a tiny minority bounced back, indicating that the foil was mainly empty space except for extraordinarily small particles that were very dense? Or did we need to see it with our own eyes? It depends on your standard of proof. If researchers were not interested in validating their hypothesis there is little chance that an electron microscope would ever have been built. We can be assured that those at the forefront of the mystery had been convinced that they were on the right track while the rest of us were shrugging our shoulders waiting for "evidence".

An even more interesting contemplation is: "Did atoms exist a thousand years ago before we were aware of such things?". We may be quick to answer, "Of course! Atoms have always existed. We know that **now!**". However isn't it also true that in order for something to exist, we must be aware of it? If that is not immediately obvious, try to name something that exists that you are not aware of. From this perspective it is not unreasonable to assert that there were no atoms then because *there was no one around who knew about them.* For example, let's say that tomorrow we find out that all of this, our world, our struggles and successes are just part of an elaborate virtual reality training game we have forgotten that we were playing. Whether this experience is "real" or a game makes no difference; today it is absolutely real because that is how we are thinking about it. We are constantly making our reality by the way we are conceiving it. If atoms had yet to be conceived where would they have existed? Only in a world defined by minds that were aware of such things. No such minds were around a thousand years ago.

For thousands of generations the night skies were often thought to be a large canopy with countless perforations hung at an arbitrary distance and backlit by heavenly light. Almost overnight we came to the understanding that the stars were in fact self-luminous, enormous and staggeringly far away. Did the universe instantaneously expand the moment we looked into a telescope for the first time? Practically speaking, *it did.*

Imagine yourself living in Italy four centuries ago looking up at the constellation of Orion the Hunter. Orion's right shoulder is the star Betelgeuse. We now know that Betelgeuse is an enormous star, millions of times bigger than the Sun by volume. If we replaced the Sun with Betelgeuse it would swallow the Earth, Mars and possibly even Jupiter. At the time you and everyone else in your world did not know what a star really was. You were just looking at a pale orange point of light probably a few hundred miles away--after all, that is about the range of what we can see from our position to another point on the surface of the Earth. There would be no reason to assume that anything, including the lights in the sky, were much farther away. One day someone you trust tells you that that point of light is another sun much bigger than ours sitting about 14 *trillion* times further away than you had thought your whole life.

Before contemplating this it is worthwhile to get an idea of what it means to expand something to that degree. These words you are reading now are appearing on a screen or a page about two feet away from you; if they were 14 trillion times farther from you they would be sitting outside the orbit of Neptune and proportionally, that much bigger. How would it *feel* the moment it sunk in? It wouldn't be any different than witnessing everything above you *actually* fly away to incomprehensible distances in a blink of an eye.

Try as we might, we cannot escape the fact that we live in a reality that we have defined in our minds alone. The bounds and intricacies of our universe are not in a state of flux because they are changing constantly as much as our *awareness* of them is evolving. Our understanding of what *is* is naturally in a state of flux. It is only when we slip into long periods of complacency about our understanding do we suffer the jarring whiplash of a paradigm shift that will inevitably come.

In this sense there are no *absolute, immutable* facts about the world around us, at least none that we can be aware of or articulate precisely. If you believe that you are aware of such a fact, how certain are you that in a hundred million years it will continue to stand true? Our understanding of everything is always subject to change; the best we can hope for is to have a good approximation of what the truth is. In that sense we live in our *narratives* about our world--and that's okay. The great thing about narratives is that you can edit them to achieve a "more perfect" (and more useful) story. However because narratives are subject to change they can be potentially manipulated. Change your narrative and you change your world. Control someone else's narrative and you control *their* world. This is how it works. This is why eliminating bias and engaging our intuition and objectivity is so vitally important.

Elephants raised in captivity are chained to stakes in the ground when they are very young to keep them from running away while unattended. Though they initially pull at their chains, young elephants can never wrench themselves free. You might think that as they grow, bigger chains and deeper stakes are required to contain them. That isn't necessary. At some point early in their life they stop pulling on their chains because they have learned that it is futile. By the time they are full grown these magnificent, intelligent animals could easily run free from the restraints that are designed to hold a much smaller version of themselves. They never do. By this point their *minds* have been contained.

Unlike in the Dark Ages where our narratives were enforced through overt methods like the threat of physical punishment, today our narratives are being authored in a way that only a very alert mind can *fully* appreciate. Notice that by advancing a narrative of fear and security through unavoidable wars it creates resistance to accepting the idea that we are naturally cooperative and that peace is attainable, not just for a few months but indefinitely. Similarly, by suppressing the possible truth that as conscious beings we have an innate compassion for each other and a natural ability to cooperate we more readily accept the fact that war is an unavoidable result of our "human nature". In that sense, *pushing* a potentially false narrative about 9/11 would condition us in the same way that *suppressing a* potentially true narrative about an ExtraTerrestrial presence on this planet does. One narrative confirms our belligerent nature while the other would suggest the potential for the opposite. When we subscribe to one it biases us against any evidence that supports the other which in turn biases us towards accepting evidence of the first. This cognitive "feedback loop" powered by *Source of Bias #8 (Confirmation Bias)* puts us in a precarious position when we approach these two narratives together because what may be initially a slight bias can become an entrenched position over time.

That same relationship exists between the possible truth of our own limitless existence and a monetary system that keeps us locked in an endless pursuit to attain the unattainable in a limited lifetime. By exaggerating the importance of keeping up with the Jones' we minimize the potential of examining our life from an expanded perspective. When the "You only live once!" narrative gets pushed we become less likely to even entertain the possibility that death is not really our demise but in fact a transcending event in our existence that we have yet to fully define. Those who eschew materialism or a competitive attitude are often at the fringes of society. They are not the movers and shakers. Instead they are portrayed as "under achievers" and "non-contributors" who have foolishly thrown away their only shot at happiness and success out of indolence. We thus become more willing to participate in a scheme that in truth extracts a great deal from us and pays enormous dividends to the tiniest of minorities. Once again, promoting one narrative while suppressing its counterpart serves to reinforce a single paradigm. Are these narratives being manipulated too? Notably the same extreme minority benefit greatly when the vast majority comply with the narratives that are in place today.

There also could be a very real link between the central banking system and the events of 9/11. The nearly endless state of war we are in unavoidably generates an extraordinary amount of wealth for the banking system. That's the way the system is set up. Therefore we cannot overlook the possibility that a nameless few behind the banking system may very well be behind the events that propel us into war. When we look away from the workings of the monetary system we are less likely to see 9/11 from a broader context. Similarly, a planet-wide acknowledgement of an ET presence on this planet (if it does exist) would potentiate a sincere exploration into our own consciousness and the limitations that we have placed on it by default. Maybe the little green men aren't neighbors with fancier gadgets. Maybe they are an advanced version of ourselves that we could embody tomorrow if we embraced a different understanding of who we are as conscious beings today.

We have explored four foundational narratives in this book. The first three, death, money and war are rarely considered to be narratives, even in a loose sense of the word. They are most often thought of as absolutes, unavoidable certainties of the human experience. The fourth, an ExtraTerrestrial presence on this planet, seems at the surface to be a recent phenomenon or just an element of fringe culture that has emerged in the last few decades, a far cry from a guiding force behind our species' trajectory like the other three. We may very well be forced to reconsider the significance of this phenomenon. ETs, if they are here, invite us to consider just how certain the first three really are. In any case, these narratives are intimately connected. They are pieces of a puzzle that interlock to construct a broader view of reality we hold in our minds collectively that reads something like this:

> Our existence is fragile and limited. We are under constant threat from enemies that seek to harm us. The only sensible approach is to protect ourselves by tapping our future efforts through a banking system that can also help us feel prosperous today. Seeing it differently is naive.

In one way or another we collectively buy into this general story, or at the very least accept it with little or no protest. This is how the world is presented to us directly and indirectly. My intention in writing this book is to invite you to consider the possibility that the pieces of this puzzle form a different picture. You needn't rearrange the pieces. Instead I invite you to flip the puzzle over and see if a completely different image presents itself. Is it worthwhile to look? What do we have to lose? How does it compare with what might be gained? Have our minds been constrained by chains we cannot see? Perhaps they have been in full view all along disguised as safety ropes to keep us from falling from precipices that do not exist.

At the end of Chapter 4 I pointed out that the simplest, most elegant solution is usually the most valid one. This general principle, Occam's Razor, is very often valid, however it is only correctly applied if **all** observations are taken into consideration. There is no utility in arriving at an elegant explanation that does not explain the totality of what is observed. We can assume that the 25% in the National Science Foundation poll who still believe the Sun orbits the Earth feel that way because there is no real need to reassess their position. An Earth-centered solar system is an elegant model of what they observe everyday. Are we being duped into misconceptions about death, money, war and isolation because we are not looking hard enough? At the surface it is not so hard to accept that death is the end, that our banking system is necessary, that two planes razed three skyscrapers and that UFO sightings are the product of overactive imaginations or just a passing curiosity. Are these adequate models of reality or are we in fact validating them because they happen to be simpler than those offered here? *How much attention are we really paying to all the details?*

We may differ in religion and political ideology (and apparently even in our understanding of the relationship between the sun and the Earth) but most of us accept the fact that we have a limited existence, that we may eventually acquire desirable things in our life through labor and the assistance of our lending institutions and that we must protect ourselves and way of life from other members of our own species who seem hell-bent on destroying us and the truths that we hold to be "self-evident". Our scientists have incrementally pushed our technology forward, allowing us to barely dip our toes into an interstellar ocean and more often than not extend our life to a ninth decade. Though this kind of world may seem acceptable (if not unavoidable) to most, is it an accurate representation of reality? Can we write a better narrative or are we being told, directly or not, that doing so would be futile or dangerous if not impossible?

Few of us live with no fear of death. We consider it to be a termination of our existence. Looking at it openly, we have no proof that our body's death is our demise, nor do we have proof that it isn't. Perhaps we consider such things as an "afterlife" in our places of worship but why do we, in general, *behave* as if there is none? Would we be attempting to out-maneuver each other to maximize our own wealth and safety if we viewed our lives more as one step of a much larger journey? Is it even possible to live in such a paradigm if we are being constantly reminded of the horrific ways a human being can die, the worst of them being at the hands of each other? To avoid such violence we are told that wars must be waged. How sensible a strategy is that? How often do people have a real opportunity to consider such things in a world that keeps us either worried over our physical and financial security or preoccupied in limitless distraction?

When we tie our own individual existence to a finite period of time we cannot help being fearful, especially when the spectre of death and illness seem to loom closer. It also engenders a more aggressive mentality when resources, especially time, are seen as limited. This perspective blinds us to bigger possibilities. If an individual assumes they will exist for no more than a century under the best of circumstances how can they be expected to consider what the impact of their choices would be over the course of a few million years? What should our expectations be for a planet of 7 billion people who all feel and act this way? With the mindset we have adopted there is only a slim possibility that we would ever make any real progress over that period of time. The best that we can reasonably hope for is that we will go in circles and not self-annihilate.

For over 70 years we have been told over and over that our world is only a few missteps from a planetary disaster. Perhaps we are on the brink of something very different: a planetary awakening. If there were such a thing in the offing, how would it be revealed to us? A televised press conference? No. The kind of shift we are talking about here is not something that we would be told about or shown. It would be something that we *feel* and know for ourselves *intuitively.* An awakening of this nature will have nothing to do with accepting someone else's narrative; it will be quite the opposite. It will be a fundamental transformation that occurs independently from within, not from without. It will be borne of an understanding that we have been lulled into abdicating authorship of our narratives to third parties not realizing that we have always had the power to write our own.

Our understanding of prosperity, conflict, life and death, and our purpose on this planet define our reality at the most fundamental level. Should prosperity be measured by the number of shells we possess? Is war truly unavoidable? How would we repurpose our lives if we became aware of other highly intelligent beings that were visiting or possibly sharing this planet with us largely silently and invisibly? If death is not the end, how then should we be living? How would our priorities change if we realized that we are inextricably connected to the fate of our planet and species even after the death of our bodies?

The answers to these questions, as always, are up to you. If there were a conclusion to be drawn it would be that we are unequivocally being told that these questions are not worth asking. Entertaining such lofty possibilities is often thought of as ungrounded or naive. But which perspective is more short-sighted? Who is being naive? Do we prosper when we remain "grounded", or does someone else benefit when we remain tied to stakes in the ground?

Perhaps you agree with the narratives that we are being subjected to daily. Perhaps the narratives are an insult to your intuition. The vitally important truth is that we have and have always had a choice to accept or reject what we have been told. This freedom to choose is perhaps the most fundamental and undeniable aspect of reality and one that we must consider very carefully. Whether you are guided by faith, objective reasoning, intuition or some of all three you are always choosing your narrative and by doing so, your reality.

I admit that I have granted "alternative" perspectives a lot of voice in this book. Though the book could be judged as an unbalanced summary of these topics, this was the unavoidable result of making a sober assessment of the lens through which we are looking. The counter arguments to those offered here are available to you at any time on all mainstream media platforms.

In writing this book I have sought to raise questions and purposefully not provide concrete answers. The fact is, there are no concrete answers to the questions I have posed. Here is where the book veers from this pattern. Having read this far I can assume that you are interested in knowing the facts and not just a story that fits your needs. This is where I finally deliver. If there is such a thing as an immutable fact it does not have to do with gravity, money, life, death, war or Extraterrestrials; it has to do with truth itself and how to identify it:

> *When truth arises, it is never disguised as an ultimatum,*
> *a ticket to exclusivity or a means of manipulation. Truth always*
> *appears as a gift to those who are ready to receive it. When you*
> ***know*** *this to be true from your own experience it will stand as*
> *your proof that reality itself is compassionate.*

INDEX

(Find these links at https://www.madhavasettymd.com)

Chapter 4

[1]   (National Science Foundation poll)
      https://www.npr.org/sections/thetwo-way/2014/02/14/277058739/1-in-4-
      americans-think-the-sun-goes-around-the-earth-survey-says

Chapter 5

[2]   (Scientific American on Dr. Stevenson)
      https://blogs.scientificamerican.com/bering-in-mind/ian-
      stevensone28099s-case-for-the-afterlife-are-we-e28098skepticse28099-
      really-just-cynics/

[3]   (Washington Post on Dr. Stevenson)
      https://www.washingtonpost.com/archive/lifestyle/magazine/1999/08/08/a-
      matter-of-death-38/edcd9cc4-e7c6-47c3-82d7-7298165a101d/

Chapter 6

[4]   (German government's warning to the American People in Des Moines
      Register)
      https://www.google.com/imgres?imgurl=http://foolscrow.files.wordpress.
      com/2014/05/lusitania-notice.jpg&imgrefurl=https://www.globalresearch.
      ca/the-sinking-the-lusitania-americas-entry-into-world-war-i-a-bonanza-
      for-wall-street/5381121&tbnid=rIo3s-DFMJVKaM&vet=1&docid=ll5nBg
      WipeFQGM&w=375&h=429&q=des+moines+register+lusitania&source=
      sh/x/im

Chapter 7

[5]   (Governor George Pataki on CNN: Where did the buildings go?)
      https://www.youtube.com/watch?v=MDuBi8KyOhw&feature=youtu.be

[6]   (Slow motion collapse of North Tower)
      https://www.youtube.com/watch?v=nUDoGuLpirc

[7]   (Map of human remains surrounding Ground Zero from FDNY via Village
      Voice)
      https://www.villagevoice.com/2010/09/10/the-posts-map-of-human-
      remains-at-ground-zero-and-the-culture-of-fear/

[8]   (NY Times: Challenge of Medical Examiners after 9/11)
      https://www.nytimes.com/2002/07/14/nyregion/at-morgue-ceaselessly-
      sifting-9-11-traces.html

[9]   (CNN: Fires at ground zero extinguished three months later)
      http://edition.cnn.com/2001/US/12/20/rec.athome.facts/index.html

[10] (Footage of Building 7 Collapse)
      https://www.youtube.com/watch?v=Mamvq7LWqRU&feature=youtu.be

[11] (University of Alaska study proving Building 7 destruction was NOT due to
      fires)
      http://ine.uaf.edu/wtc7

[12] (CSPAN : Sec. State Rumsfeld and Joint Chief of Staff Chair confirm
      NORAD exercises on morning of 9/11)
      https://www.youtube.com/watch?v=Px1t1-a9uxk

[13] (Third Party analysis of the collapse sequence of twin towers from Journal
      of Engineering Mechanics formulated two days after 9/11)
      http://www-math.mit.edu/~bazant/WTC/WTC-asce.pdf

[14] (Official NIST document referencing weight of top section of North
      Tower—see table on page 176)
      http://www.911facts.dk/resources/NIST/NCSTAR_1-6D.pdf

[15] (Slow motion collapse of North Tower—there is no top section of North
      Tower)
      https://www.youtube.com/watch?v=nUDoGuLpirc

[16] (Molten metal spewing from South Tower after plane collision)
      https://www.youtube.com/watch?v=dYfMzqHouuI

[17] (FDNY Captain describes molten steel flowing in the basement of twin
      tower)
      https://www.youtube.com/watch?v=nsw2j-3MCMg&feature=youtu.be

[18] (Summary of testimony from 118 Firefighters confirming explosive events prior to the collapse of the twin towers) http://www.journalof911studies.com/articles/Article_5_118Witnesses_WorldTradeCenter.pdf

[19] (Multiple mainstream media reports of explosions in twin towers) https://www.youtube.com/watch?v=YULx2_4zKSM

[20] (Organization of Firefighters calling for reinvestigation of 9/11) https://www.ff911truth.org

[21] (Super slow motion clip of the beginning of North Tower collapse:antenna moves first) https://www.youtube.com/watch?v=jBh7jHltdSs

[22] (Cover of Elevator World magazine confirming massive elevator renovation in twin towers prior to 9/11) http://911research.wtc7.net/cache/wtc/arch/wtc_elevator_renovation.pdf

[23] (Previously classified documents regarding project Northwoods from 1962. Page 10 of Annex to Appendix to Enclosure A describes a proposed scenario similar to 9/11) https://nsarchive2.gwu.edu/news/20010430/northwoods.pdf

[24] (Organization of professional pilots requesting reinvestigation of 9/11) http://pilotsfor911truth.org

[25] (Transcript of President G.W. Bush address to the U.N. in 11/2001 invoking the term "Conspiracy Theory" seven years before the conclusion of the official investigation) https://www.americanrhetoric.com/speeches/gwbush911unitednations.htm

[26] (Organization of professional Architects and Engineers calling for reinvestigation of 9/11) https://www.ae911truth.org

[27] (Webinars designed by Architects to inform other professionals about the deficiencies in the official investigation) https://www.ae911truth.org/evidence/videos/category/28-9-11-an-architect-s-guide-three-part-webinar

[28] (BBC original broadcast announcing the destruction of Building 7 20 minutes before the event) https://www.youtube.com/watch?v=OI6D0ZZ0kzo

[29] (CNN coverage from the ground moments before the destruction of Building 7. Police stating the building is about to blow up) https://www.youtube.com/watch?v=cU_43SwWD9A&feature=youtu.be

Chapter 8

[30] (CBS reports US Navy pilots confirm UFOs over East Coast) https://www.cbsnews.com/news/navy-pilots-ufo-reports-confirmed-new-york-times-military-unidentified-flying-object/

[31] (CNN reports US Navy acknowledges UFO footage) https://www.cnn.com/2019/09/18/politics/navy-confirms-ufo-videos-trnd/index.html

[32] (Dr. Greer, FAA and ex military officials announce that UFOs are real at National Press Club in 2001) https://vimeo.com/ondemand/nationalpressclub2001

[33] (Sirius Disclosure Website) https://siriusdisclosure.com

[34] (Trinity, first detonation of a nuclear device on Earth) https://en.wikipedia.org/wiki/Trinity_(nuclear_test)

[35] (Joe Rogan interviews Bob Lazar) https://www.youtube.com/watch?v=TiGbn0rck1E

[36] (Invention Secrecy Act) https://en.wikipedia.org/wiki/Invention_Secrecy_Act

[37] (Patent Security Category Review List from 1971) https://fas.org/sgp/othergov/invention/pscrl.pdf